French

Learn French For Beginners Including French Grammar, French Short Stories and 1000+ French Phrases

Contents

Part 1: French

An Essential Guide to French Language Learning

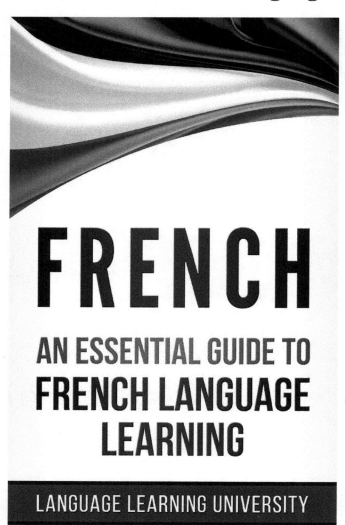

INTRODUCTION

French is currently one of the most widely used languages on the international scene. It is an official language in 29 countries.

Do you want to learn French quickly? There is no miracle recipe; you have to start with the basics. Or perhaps you already know the basics, but you still have difficulties in assimilating this charming language. Do not worry; you're not alone.

Perhaps this is the first book that introduces you to the French language, or you have already read others, but you have given up. Rest assured, you will learn to speak in a simple and clear way, just like me when I started with this rich language that is French. French tends to have a reputation among English speakers as hard to learn, but it's easier than you might think. Many courses of language study assume you are going to a particular location for vacation, and so the lessons begin with everyday survival phrases that people use. There is some of that in this book; however, consider that it is "verbs" that make a language. It's important to learn the language in a broader sense as well.

During each chapter, you will be taught the fundamentals of the language, and each part will be illustrated with examples, followed by practical exercises.

If you want to learn the basics of French for speaking, reading, and writing, you'll need to learn each chapter in the order they are presented.

Here is your first book on French, and its objective is simple:

To introduce you to the French language.

CHAPTER 1 - PRONUNCIATION

Learning a language in its written form is easy. The hardest part is to assimilate pronunciation, because each language has its own phonetic sound.

Indeed, some pronunciations are unique to the French language and do not exist in English. When you start learning French, the pronunciations can seem tricky. This is especially the case because it has a lot of sounds that don't exist in English. However, French pronunciation does not have to be difficult.

1.1 The French alphabet

The French alphabet looks very similar to the English alphabet, but there are a few differences. There is a total of 26 letters in the French alphabet. Standard French contains 13 oral vowels and up to 4 nasal vowels, but there are also 5 additional accented letters that can be applied to change the sound of a letter.

The words between [...] are phonetics in English.

a A [*Ah*]	n N [hun]
b B [*Ba(y)*]	o O [Oh]
c C [*Sa(y)*]	p P [Pay]
d D [*Da(y)*]	q Q [Coo]
e E [*Uh*]	r R [err]
f F [ayf]	s S [ess]
g G [zhay]	t T [tay]
h H [Ash]	u U[u]
i I [Eeh]	v V [vay]
j J[zhee]	w W[doub-leh-vey-]
k K [kah]	x X [eeks]
l L [ell]	y Y [ee-grek]
m M [hum]	z Z [zed]

1.1.1 Vowels, consonants, and their combination

Vowels:

A e i u o y

Consonants:

B c d f g h j k l m m n p q r s t v w x y z

The French "R" is pronounced "Errr," as when you are about to spit. This is the best example to describe its sonority because only a few languages use the famous French "R" sound. When you attempt to pronounce it correctly, people will see that you're trying, so they'll be willing to help and encourage you. Keep practicing, softening it up a bit each time. It's similar to a Spanish "J" sound.

The "Y" is pronounced as "ee" in English.

The "H" is silent in French; it does not accentuate the word that contains it.

The Silent "h"

The "h" in French is a 100% silent letter no matter where it's located in a word. The only exception to this is when the preceding letter is "c," in which case the "ch" combination makes a "sh" sound or "k" sound.

"Housse" (Cover), for example, is pronounced "Ouss."

"Chaos" sounds like "Kaoh."

Single "s," Double "s" or "z"?

But it's just an "s," right? Pronouncing the "s" is more complicated than it seems. The double "S" or "Ss" is pronounced like the end of the word "Bass," for example.

The simple "S" is pronounced like "Poison."

The difference between "é" "ait" and "et"

When you speak the following sentences, does the conjugation of the verb "parler" sound the same?

- J'ai parlé avec lui

- Je parlais avec lui

Many French learners will pronounce these in exactly the same way, but they should not sound the same. This is surprising, but true.

"é" and "et" are pounounced "eh," while "Ait" or "ais" are pronounced like "May" with the "y" sound at the end.

1.2 Combination of vowels

The combination of vowels in French gives a different sound that does not exist in the English language.

Ai [eh]

Ue [uay]

Oi [wah]

Oui [wee]

Ui [uee]

1.2.1 Combination of consonants with consonants

The combination of consonants with consonants is pronounced as in English (cl, gu, qu etc ...), except for the following:

Ch [Shuh] but not Tch

Tr [Trrr] but not Tchr

1.2.2 Combination of vowels with consonants

We have seen the combinations of vowels with vowels; here we shall see the combinations of vowels with consonants. Why? Because their sound is different from English. They are combinations that are used in almost every word in French.

Ail ille eil [ahy], [eey], [ayy]

On [On] (The "N" is silent. We do not pronounce it, we just keep the sound of the "o" in English.)

Dropping the L in Your "il" and Your "elle"

Pronouncing your "il" and "elle" like French speakers is easier than pronouncing it the "proper" way, and is an effective way to make your colloquial speech sound much more natural.

Consider the following two sounds:

ee-lee-ya

ee-ya

Say each sound aloud several times in a row. Which one can you say more quickly and easily? When it comes to the phrase "il y a," French speakers simplify it to sound like "ee-ya." Following are a couple of examples:

- Est-ce qu'il y a quelqu'un? (Is there someone out there?)

- Oui, il y a quelqu'un. (Yes, there is.)

It doesn't end there, however. In everyday French conversation, particularly when you're speaking quickly, you can drop the l from "il" and "elle" in the majority of sentences. This is particularly the case when the next word in the sentence starts with a consonant. Here are some examples:

- Qu'est-ce qu'il fait? ("skee" fait)

- Elle connait mon frère ("eh" connait)

- Il veut ça ("kee" veut)

- Je veux qu'elle réponde à mes appels ("keh" réponde)

Two of the most well known are the silent "e" and the silent "h."

There is, however, an exception for the silent "e."

1.3 Masculine and Feminine

The silent final "e" poses an interesting situation when it comes to masculine and feminine words. In the case of feminine adjectives and nouns, this typically means that the final consonant of the masculine form will now be pronounced.

Ex.:

Charmant-Charmante

Aimant-Aimante

le chat / la chatte

The (male) cat / The (female) cat

"u" or "ou"?

In addition to the "u," there's also the "ou," which is pronounced slightly differently. Making a distinction between the two is important. In order to pronounce the "ou," all you need to do is think "soup."

The French language isn't written phonetically. The same sound can be represented by several different combinations of letters.

The French language also uses *liaison* which is the pronunciation of a latent word-final consonant right before a following vowel sound. Liaisons are a phonetic link between two words that may sound awkward for native speakers if left unconnected. Let's take a look at some examples:

Vous

You

Vous êtes (Voozhet)

You are

You'll automatically be able to notice where a liaison is needed and how to make it sound natural with practice.

One of the fundamental rules of pronouncing French is that everything has to flow. If you're speaking French correctly, everything should sound as if it comes out beautifully.

1.4 The Final Consonant

Many French letters simply aren't pronounced at the end of words. In general, the final consonants of a word are usually silent in French except in some cases of the letters c, f, l or r.

Let's take a look at some examples of silent consonants at the end of words.

froid (Frwaa)

cold

Grand (Grhun)

big/large

Beaucoup (Bokoo)

a lot/many/much

Petit (Puhtee)

Little

Exercise:

Now let's try an exercise to help us practice pronunciation.

Aide-moi [Ehd mwah]

Voici ma famille [Vwahsea mah fahmeey]

Il y a une oie là bàs [Ill ee ah unh wah labah]

Le patron me cherche [Luh pahtRon me cherche]

Repeat these phrases to get used to the pronunciation of French words. For now, you do not need to know their meaning; we are just working on pronunciation.

1.5 French numbers

1.5.1 Cardinal numbers

The words between (...) or [...] are phonetics in English

1	11
Un (un)	Onze (onze)
2	12
Deux (deh)	Douze (dooze)
3	13
Trois (trwah)	Treize (TREH-z)
4	14
Quatre(KAH-trah)	Quatorze (KAH-torze)
5	15
Cinq (sank)	Quinze (KAH-nz)
6	16
Six (seez)	Seize (SEH-z)
7	17
Sept (set)	Dix-sept (DEE-set)
8	18
Huit (wheet)	Dix-huit (DEEZ-wheet)
9	19
Neuf (nehf)	Dix-neuf (DEEZ-nehf)
10	20
Dix (deez)	Vingt (van)

This is how to count the numbers after twenty.

21	vingt et un	[vant-ay-uh]
22	vingt-deux	[van-duhr]
23	vingt-trois	[van-twa]
24	vingt-quatre	[van-katr]
25	vingt-cinq	[van-sank]
26	vingt-six	[van-sees]
27	vingt-sept	[van-set]
28	vingt-huit	[van-weet]
29	vingt-neuf	[van-nurf]
30	Trente	[tront]
31	Trente et un	[tront ay-uh]
40	quarante	[karont]
50	cinquante	[sank-ont]
60	soixante	[swa-sont]
70	soixante-dix	[swa-sont-dees]
80	quatre-vingts	[kat-ra-van]
90	quatre-vingt-dix	[kat-ra-van-dees]
100	Cent	[son]

Note: In French, the numbers one to ten are the base. Now you just have to remember twenty, thirty etc., to which you will then add the 1-10 digits to complete.

Ex.:

51	cinquante et un	[sank-ont-ay-uh]
52	cinquante-deux	[sank-ont-deux]
53	cinquante-trois	[sank-ont-twa]

54	cinquante-quatre	[sank-ont-katr]
55	cinquante-cinq	
56	cinquante-six	[sank-ont-sank]
57	cinquante-sept	[sank-ont-sees]
58	cinquante-huit	[sank-ont-set]
59	cinquante-neuf	[sank-ont-weet]
60	soixante	[sank-ont-nurf]
		[swa-sont]

Then for soixante it would be soixante-et-un or 61, soixante-et-deux or 62, soixante-et-trois ou 63, and so on.

Note: All tens are counted by adding and-one, and-two, and-three, and-four, etc., except 70 and 90, which are exceptions.

There it would be 60 and 11, or sixty and eleven, sixty and twelve, and so on

Once you memorize the base numbers, all other numbers are just combinations.

Ex :

70	soixante-dix	[swa-sont-dees]
71	soixante-et-onze	[swa-sont-ay-onz]
72	soixante-douze	
73	soixante-treize	[swa-sont-dooz]
74	soixante-quatorze	[swa-sont-trez]
		[swa-sont-katorz]
75	soixante-quinze	
76	soixante-seize	[swa-sont-kanz]
77	soixante-dix-sept	[swa-sont-sez]
		[swa-sont-dee-set]
78	soixante-dix-	

	huit	
79	soixante-dix-neuf	[swa-sont-dees-weet]
		[swa-sont-dees-nurf]

For 90, you would say : "quatre-vingt-dix," which means " "four twenty and ten." You have to use the same process you use for 70.

Ex.:

90	quatre-vingt-dix	[kat-ra-van-dees]
91	quatre-vingt-onze	[kat-ra-van-onz]
92	quatre-vingt-douze	[kat-ra-van-dooz]
93	quatre-vingt-treize	[kat-ra-van- trez]

Note: Mille (1 000) is never plural, but multiples of million are, even if they don't end the written number.

A number ending in one can agree in gender with whatever it's modifying. The story "1,001 Nights" is translated as "Mille-et-une Nuits" since nuit is feminine.

Just as we do not say "one over two" for "a half" in English, neither do the French. Here are some common French fractions.

1/2 — un demi

une demi-tasse — half a cup

trois ans et demi — three and a half years

1/3 — un tiers

1/4 — un quart

1/5 — un cinquième

1/10 — un dixième

1/100 — un centième

If *un* (one) is the last word in a phrase, it doesn't agree in gender with the preceding noun. So we say, "*la page* **un**" and not "*la page une*" for "page 1."

1.5.2 Ordinal numbers

For ordinal numbers, the formula is simple.

The ordinal numbers in English are "first," "second," "third," etc. This is easy in French. With the exception of premier/première (first), you just tack on –ième to a number to turn it into an ordinal number.

Ex.:

French	Abbreviation	Phonetic	Meaning
Premier (used to refer to a masculine noun)	1er	Pruhmeeai	First
Première (used to refer to a feminine noun)	1ère	Pruhmeeerr	First
French	Abbreviation	Phonetic	Meaning
Deuxième Troisième Quatrième Cinquième	2ème 3ème 4ème 5ème	Duhzyaim Trwahzyaim KAH-treeaim sankeeaim	Second Third Fourth Fifth

Repeat them until you no longer hesitate when you read them.

Basic vocabulary related to numbers and math:

To add — additionner/ajouter

To subtract — retrancher/soustraire

To multiply — multiplier

To divide — diviser

Sum — somme (f)/montant (m)

Difference — différence (f)

Product — produit (m)

Quotient — quotient

To equal — égaler

Integer — entier (m)

Prime number — nombre premier (m)

Given (in math parlance) — soit

CHAPTER 2 - TIME, DATES, AND CALENDAR

2.1 The time

Telling time in French is not complicated. It's a little bit different from English, but you just need to know the French numbers, and a few formulas and rules.

The French word for "time" is "Heure," not "le temps" (Literally).

In English, we often leave out "o'clock." It's perfectly fine to say, "It's nine" or "I'm waking up at 6." That is not so in French. You always have to say "HEURE" after every number, except with "Midi" (Noon) and 'Minuit" (Midnight).

In French, the hour and minute are separated by an "h" (abbreviation of heure).

Ex.:

15 h30

12h12

How to say it?

What Time Is It?	*Quelle heure est-il?*
It's one o'clock	*Il est une heure (1h)*
It's two o'clock	*Il est deux heures (2h)*

Telling time in French would be, "It is one hour, two hour, three hour," and so on.

The French language doesn't have words for "a.m." and "p.m." You can use "du matin" (of the morning) for a.m., "de l'après-midi" (of the afternoon) from noon until about 6 p.m., and "du soir" (of the evening) from 6 p.m. until midnight, at the end of your sentence. However, time is usually expressed on a 24-hour clock.

There are two ways to count time in French.

In English, it would be 12 o'clock-12 o'clock, but in French, there are two possibilities.

From 12h (Douze heures or Noon), French people continue with the following:

13h 00

14h 00

15h 00

16h 00

17h 00

18h 00

19h 00 etc.

3 p.m. is normally expressed as *quinze heures* or *15h00*, but you can also say *trois heures (3h) de l'après-midi (afternoon)*. Either way is acceptable.

Reading the Time:

What time is it?	*Quelle heure est-il?*	*Abbreviations*
Morning/AM	Il est zéro heure	Il est 0h00.
	Il est une heure	Ils est 1h00
	Il est deux heures	Il est 2h00
	Il est trois heures	Il est 3h00.
	Il est quatre heures	Il est 4h00.

This continues until 12 heures or Midi (noon).

What time is it?	*Quelle heure est-il?*	*Abbreviations*
Afternoon/PM	Il est douze heures or Midi	Il est 12h00.
	Il est treize heures	Ils est 13h00
	Il est quatorze heures	Il est 14h00

French "p.m." ends at 23h 00. After 23 h00, it's not 24 h00 but 0h00.

Telling time in French (quarter, half etc…)

It's 3:30	Il est trois heures et Demi or Il est trois heures trente	3h30
It's 5:15	Il est cinq heures et quart Il est cinq heures quinze	5h15
It's 4:45	Il est cinq heures moins le quart or Il est cinq heures moins quinze or Il est quatre heures quarante-cinq	4h45

Time of the day

lever du soleil	sunrise
aube	dawn
matin, matinée	morning
midi	noon
après-midi	afternoon
soirée, soir [Am]	evening
crépuscule	dusk
nuit	night
minuit	midnight

Asking for the time

Expressions

Quelle heure est-il ?

Est-ce que vous avez l'heure, s'il vous plaît ?

English	French
When did you get here?	Quand est-ce que tu es arrivé ici ?
Today	Aujourd'hui
Yesterday	Hier
October	Octobre
November	Novembre
December	Décembre
What time are you leaving at?	Tu pars à quelle heure ?
Morning, at eight o'clock	Le matin, à huit heures
Morning, at quarter past 8	Le matin, à huit heures quinze
Morning, at half past 8	Le matin, à huit heures trente
Morning, at a quarter to nine	Le matin, à huit heures quarante cinq
Evening, at 6pm	Le soir, à dix-huit heures
I am late.	Je suis en retard

2.2 Days of the week

Lundi   Monday

Mardi   Tuesday

Mercredi   Wednesday

Jeudi   Thursday

Vendredi   Friday

Samedi   Saturday

Dimanche Sunday

Expressions

Quel jour est-il?

What day is it?

Or Quel jour sommes-nous?

Nous sommes Dimanche

Or just

C'est Dimanche.

2.2 Dates

The date is really simple in French.

It is pronounced just after the day (Lundi, Mardi, Vendredi etc.) and "Le" is put before the day.

Ex.:

Quel jour sommes-nous ?

What day is it?

Nous sommes **le** *Mardi* **15** Aout 2017.

We are on Tuesday 15 August 2017.

We use the ordinal number "1er" or "Premeier" only for the first day of the month..

Expressions

Day	jour; journée
Week	Semaine
Fortnight	Quinzaine
Month	Mois
Monthly	Mensuel
Quarter	quart, trimester
Year	an, année
Leapyear	année bissextile
Century	siècle
The day before yesterday	avant-hier
Yesterday	hier
Today	aujourd'hui, de nos jours
Tomorrow	demain
The day after tomorrow	après-demain

2.4 Calendar

2.4.1 Months of the year

Janvier	January
Février	February
Mars	March
Avril	April
Mai	May
Juin	June
Juillet	July
Août	August
Septembre	September
Octobre	October
Novembre	November
Décembre	December

Note: Days and months are always capitalized.

2.4.2 Seasons

Printemps	spring
Eté	summer
Automne	autumn
Automne [Am]	fall
Hiver	winter

2.4.3 Years

Asking About Years

To ask what year it is, you need the word *année.* *

Quelleannéeest-ce ? (En)Quelleannéesommes-nous?
What year is it?

C'était en quelle année ?
What year was that (in)?

Cela s'est passé en quelle année ?
What year did that happen?

En quelle année es-tu né ?   Quelle est l'année de ta naissance ?
What year were you born?

En quelle année vas-tu déménager ?   Tu vas déménager en quelle année ?
(In) What year are you going to move?

De quelle année est ce vin ?   Le vin est de quelle année ?
What year is this wine (from)?

Saying Years

When talking about what year it is or when something happened/will happen, the choice between an and année depends on the type of number you're dealing with. (Of course, if the context is obvious, you can also leave out "year" entirely.)

With round numbers (those ending in 0), you need "l'an."

C'est l'an 2010.	It's 2010.
En l'an 900.	In the year 900

With all other numbers, French also uses "l'année."

C'est l'année 2013.	It's 2013.
En l'année 1999.	In 199.

Note: In French, you have to pronounce the whole year just exactly like you would count numbers.

Ex.:

1993 Mille neuf cent quatre-vingt treize

1999 Mille neuf cent quatre-vingt-dix-neuf

1863 Mille huit cent soixante-trois

1505 Mille cinq cent cinq

1999 mille neuf cent quatre-vingt-dix-neuf**¨

1300 mille trois cents***

Era specification

av. J-C	Avant Jésus-Christ	BC	Before Christ
AEC	Avant l'ère commune	BCE	Before the Current/Common Era
ap. J-C	après Jésus-Christ	AD	Anno Domini
EC	ère commune, notre ère	CE	Current Era, Common Era

Pronouncing Years

How to say the year itself depends on the century in question. When talking about years up to and including 1099, or from 2000 and up, the year is stated the same as any other number.

752   Sept cent cinquante-deux

1099   mille quatre-vingt-dix-neuf   mil quatre-vingt-dix-neuf*

2000   Deux mille

2013   Deux mille treize

For years between 1100 and 1999, there are two equally valid options:

1)   Pronounce it like a regular number.

1999   mille neuf cent quatre-vingt-dix-neuf   mil neuf cent quatre-vingt-dix-neuf**

1863   mille huit cent soixante-trois   mil huit cent soixante-trois

1505   mille cinq cent cinq   mil cinq cent cinq

1300   mille trois cents***   mil trois cents

Use the centaines vigésimales (or vicésimales) counting system. Break the year into two pairs of two-digit numbers, and place the word "cent" between the pairs.

	Traditional Spelling	1990 SpellingRreformation
1999	dix-neuf cent quatre-vingt-dix-neuf	dix-neuf-cent-quatre-vingt-dix-neuf

1863	dix-huit cent soixante-trois	dix-huit-cent-soixante-trois
1505	quinze cent cinq	quinze-cent-cinq
1300	treize cents***	treize-cents

CHAPTER 3 – THE SENTENCE

3.1 Elements of a sentence

A sentence in French consists of a subject followed by a verb and a complement. Of course, this varies according to the complexity of the sentence. There may be additional words or adjectives, but the basic structure of a sentence in French is as follows:

Subject + Verb + **Object**

Or

Name + Verb + **Object**

This is very similar to English.

3.1.1 Subject

The subject is a person, animal, or object. A subject is either a noun or a pronoun.

There are 6 types of pronouns in the French language.

Personal subject pronouns

The personal subject pronouns designate or represent the person who speaks or the person to whom the sentence is addressed, a third person or an object.

The French language uses personal subject pronouns in almost all sentences.

Singular	Plural	Meaning
Je		I
Tu		You
Il / Elle		He/She/It
	Nous	We
	Vous	You
	Ils/Elles	They

Note: In French, "it" does not exist, because even objects or animals have their own gender. You use "Il" or "Elle" instead. "They" is represented by "Ils (Plural masculine) / Elles (plural feminine)". In English, the genre is mixed when the word is plural, but not in French.

When there are men and women, the masculine prevails, so we use "Ils."

However, when we talk about many women, we use "Elles." Whether for pronouns, conjugated verbs, or nouns, the spelling always takes into account the gender of the subject or the name that constitutes it.

Ex.:

Voilà les femmes, elles sont là. (There are the women, they are there.)

Voilà les hommes, ils sont là. (There are the men, they are there.)

Voilà les hommes et les femmes, ils sont là. (There are the men and women, they are there.)

Names

The name is a word that varies in gender and in number. There are several types of names, but they can be divided into two main categories, *proper names* and *common names*. They are usually replaced by subject personal pronouns when they are used as repetitions in a sentence.

Proper names

Proper names designate a living being. They are used without a determiner and begin with a capital letter.

Proper nouns are unique according to the nature of the subject. On the other hand, they do not vary in number.

Ex.:

Peter, Matthieu, Claudia, John, Alice …

Common nouns (Names and Nouns are the same thing)

Common nouns represent a set of things, whether animate or inanimate, and are introduced by a determiner.

In French, each person, animal, or even object has a gender (masculine or feminine), and varies according to their number (singular, plural).

Ex.:

Singular: Le chat (The cat), L'homme (The human), la table (The table)

Plural: Les chats, Les hommes, les tables

Possessive pronouns

After seeing the personal subject pronouns, it is time to see the possessive pronouns that correspond to each subject.

The French language uses possessive pronouns to designate the property of a person or the object concerned.

Possessive pronouns vary according to their number. They can switch from "Mon" (My) to "Mes" (which are always "My" in English, even in plural).

Ex.:

Mon sac (My Bag)

Pluriel- Mes sacs (My bags)

Personal pronouns	Singular	Plural
Je	Mon (My)	Mes (My)
Tu	Ton (Your)	Tes (Your)
Il/Elle	Son (His /Her)	Ses (His /Her)

Nous	Notre (Our)	Nos (Our)
Vous	Votre (Yours)	Vos (Yours)
Ils	Leur (Their)	Leurs (Their)

Exercise:

Fill the blanks with the possessive pronoun adapted to the subject, taking into account the gender and the number.

Il a perdu … livre. (He lost his book.)

Il a perdu … livres. (He lost his books.)

Tu as perdu … livre. (You lost your book.)

Tu as perdu … livres. (You lost your books.)

Voici … ami (This is my friend.)

Voici … amis (These are my friends.)

3.1.2 Verb

The verb is the pillar, or the fundamental element, to express what one wishes to say. It is the subject who gives his person and his number to a verb, but it is the verb which directs the actions of the subject or the name. It expresses an action or a state of being.

Verbs are composed of an infinitive plus a termination.

The most frequently used verbs are:

abuser (To abuse)- aimer (To like)- apprendre (To learn/To teach)- associer (To associate)- atterrir (To land)- avoir (To have)- calculer (To calculate)- commencer (To start)- consentir (To consent)- construire (To build)- coudre (To sew)- décevoir(To disappoint)- devoir (To have to)- dire (To say)- entendre (To hear)- envoyer (To send)- être (To be)- éviter (To avoid)- faire (To do)- habiller (To dress)- informer (To inform)- interrompre (To interrupt)- joindre (To match)- obtenir (To get)- passer (To pass)- pourrir (To rot)- pouvoir (To can)- prendre (To take)- relever (To raise)- réserver (To book)- retourner (To return)- réussir (To succeed)- échouer (To fail)- serrer (To hold)- sortir (To exit)- toucher (To touch)- trouver (To find)- venir (To come)-mourir (To die)-emprunter (To borrow)

What did you notice?

Some verbs end with "-er," others with "-ir," and others with "-oir."

To facilitate their conjugation, the French verbs are divided into three groups.

The verbs of the first group

The first group includes all regular verbs ending in -er except the verb "aller" (To go).

Ex.:

Abuser (To abuse)

Radical: Abus (means "abuse")

Termination: ER

Infinitive: Abus+**ER** = Abuser

The termination "ER" here replaces "To" in English.

There are different terminations in -er such as:

abuser (To abuse)- aimer (To like)- apprendre (To learn/To teach)- associer (To associate)- atterrir (To land)- avoir(To have)- calculer (To calculate)- commencer (To start)- consentir (To consent)- construire (To build)- coudre (To sew)- décevoir (To disappoint)- devoir (To have to)- dire (To say)- entendre (To hear)- envoyer (To send)- être (To be)- éviter (To avoid)- faire (To do)- habiller (To dress)- informer (To inform)- interrompre (To interupt-joindre (To match)- obtenir (To get)- passer (To pass)- pourrir (To rot)- pouvoir (To can)- prendre (To take)- relever (To raise)- réserver (To book)- retourner (To return)- réussir (To succeed)- échouer (To fail)- serrer (To hold)- sortir (To exit)- toucher (To touch)- trouver (To find)- venir (To come)- mourir (To die)- Emprunter (To borrow)

They represent almost 90% of French verbs.

The verbs of the second group

The second group includes all regular verbs ending with -ir.

Ex.:

Consentir (To consent)

Infinitive: Consent (means"consent") + IR

Termination: IR

Verb: Consent + IR = Consentir

The termination "IR" here replaces "To" in English.

abuser (To abuse)- aimer (To like)- apprendre (To learn/To teach)- associer (To associate)- atterrir (To land)- avoir (To have)- calculer (To calculate)- commencer (To start)- consentir (To consent)- construire (To build)- coudre (To sew)- décevoir(To disappoint)- devoir (To have to)- dire (To say)- entendre (To hear)- envoyer (To send)- être (To be)- éviter (To avoid)- faire (To do)- habiller (To dress)- informer (To inform)- interrompre (To interupt)- joindre (To match)- obtenir (To get)- passer (To pass)- pourrir (To rot)- pouvoir (To can)- prendre (To take)- relever (To raise)- réserver (To book)- retourner (To return)- réussir (To succeed)- échouer (To fail)- serrer (To hold)- sortir (To exit)- toucher (To touch)- trouver (To find)- venir (To come)- mourir (To die)- emprunter (To borrow)

The verbs of the third group

These are the verbs that are not in the first or second group. They are called irregular.

These are the verbs that end with -oir.

abuser (To abuse)- aimer (To like)- apprendre (To learn/To teach)- associer (To associate)- atterrir (To land)- avoir (To have)- calculer (To calculate)- commencer (To start)- consentir (To consent)- construire (To build)- coudre (To sew)- décevoir (To disappoint)- devoir (To have to)- dire (To say)- entendre (To hear)- envoyer (To send)- être (To be)- éviter (To avoid)- faire (To do)- habiller (To dress)- informer (To inform)- interrompre (To interupt)- joindre (To match - obtenir (To get)- passer (To pass)- pourrir (To rot)- pouvoir (To can)- prendre (To take)- relever (To raise)- réserver (To book)- retourner (To return)- réussir (To succeed)- échouer (To fail)- serrer (To hold)- sortir (To exit)- toucher (To touch)- trouver (To find)- venir (To come)- mourir (To die)- emprunter (To borrow)

Example 1: Avoir (To have)

Radical: Av

Termination: OIR

Infinitive: Av + OIR = Avoir

The termination "OIR" here replaces "To" in English.

These are the verbs that end in -re.

abuser (To abuse)- aimer (To like)- apprendre (To learn/To teach)- associer (To associate)- atterrir (To land) - avoir (To have)- calculer (To calculate)- commencer (To start)- consentir (To consent)- construire (To build)- coudre (To sew)- décevoir(To disappoint)- devoir (To have to)- dire (To say)- entendre (To hear)- envoyer (To send)- être (To be)- éviter (To avoid)- faire (To do)- habiller (To dress)- informer (To inform) -interrompre (To interupt)- joindre (To match)- obtenir (To get)- passer (To pass)- pourrir (To rot)- pouvoir (To can)- prendre (To take)- relever (To raise)- réserver (To book)- retourner (To return)- réussir (To succeed)- échouer (To fail)- serrer (To hold)- sortir (To exit)- toucher (To touch)- trouver (To find)- venir (To come)- mourir (To die)- mprunter (To borrow)

Example 2: Apprendre (To learn / To teach)

Radical: Apprend (means learn)

Termination: RE

Infinitive: Apprend + RE = Apprendre

The termination "RE" here replaces "To" in English.

3.2 Complements

A complement can be anywhere in a sentence. It is not part of the subject or the verb. It simply serves to enrich the sentence by giving more precision and/or more details.

There are three types of complements that we differentiate according to how they are used.

Complements describing time

J'arrive ce mois (quand? Ce mois)

I arrive this month. (when? This month)

Complements describing a location

Je t'attendrai au parc (où? Au parc)

I'll wait for you at the park. (where? At the park)

Complements describing the action

Il me l'a dit gentiment (comment ? Gentiment)

He said it kindly. (how?)

Note: Simple sentences may not contain complements; however, there may be several in a compound or complex sentence.

Ex.:

En ce moment, j'ai juste envie de rester tranquillement dans mon coin.

Right now, I just want to stay quietly in my corner.

3.3 Articles

In French, the article is used in almost every sentence. It is equivalent to "the" in English, but unlike English, each article in French varies according to its gender (masculine or feminine).

There are three categories of articles: defined articles (we know the number or quantity of the noun with which it is affiliated), indefinite articles (naming nouns in general terms, without designating someone or something in particular), and partitive articles.

Definite articles

They refer to a person or thing in a specific way.

Masculine

L'

Le

Feminine

L'

La

Note: "L'" is used before a vowel.

Singular and plural:

In French, you just have to add an "s" to the end of a word to make it plural. You add an "s" at the end of masculine articles. In the plural form, articles no longer have gender.

Plural of L', Le, La is Les.

Singular	Plural	Meaning
Le/La	Les[Lai]	The

Indefinite articles

Just like the definite articles, these designate a person or a thing, but in an imprecise way.

Singular	Plural	Meaning
Un/Une	Des	One
De	Des [Dai]	Some

Je prendrai bien un verre ce soir

I'll have a drink tonight.

(A glass, without specifying which one)

The partitive articles

They designate a part of something, without knowing which one.

Singular	Plural	Meaning
Du (De+La)	Des	Some
De la	Pas de pluriel	Some
De l'	Pas de pluriel	Some

"Du" is used before a masculine name.

Ex.:

Le vin (Wine)

Je veux boire **du** vin (I want to drink some wine.)

"De la" is used before a feminine name.

Ex.:

La soupe (Soup)

Je veux **de la** soupe

"De la" is used before the vowel "H."

Ex.:

L'évolution de l'homme (The evolution of the man.)

"De l'" is used before words beginning with a consonant.

Ex.:

Voiçi mes notes de l'année dernière. (These are my marks of last year.)

Brian est l'ami de mon frère. (Brian is my brother's friend.)

Ce Cette [Set]

De De

Masculine:

Mon

Feminine:

Ma

Que mangeons-nous ce soir ? (What do we eat tonight?)

De l'agneau (Lamb)

However, when the names are mixed (masculine and feminine subjects together), the masculine always prevails.

Ex.:

Voilà les hommes et les femmes . (Here are the men and the women.)

Les voilà ! (Here are they!)

Here "Les" is a genderless article, encompassing men and women.

Note: Articles are always placed after verbs. However, if they precede a name and are followed by an adjective, then they are determinants.

3.4 Determinants

The determinant is in the nominal group category. As we said before, they are before a name and are separated from it by an adjective. It varies in kind and in number.

There are several types of determinants.

Demonstrative determinants

They are used to identify a person or an object in a precise way.

Masculine singular	Feminine singular	Plural
ce, cet	cette	ces

Note: There are also forms composed with -ci or -là.

We use -ci to express proximity in time or space, and -there for distance.

- Masculine singular: ce...-là, ce...-ci, cet...-ci, cet...-là

- Feminine singular: cette...-ci, cette...-là
- Plural: ces...-ci, ces...-là.

Ex.:
-Ce garçon-ci est fiancé à cette fille-là.

-This boy is engaged to this girl.
-Ces enfants-là sont très bruyants.

-Those children are very noisy.

When the determiner precedes a name (or an adjective qualifying that name) that begins with a vowel or a mute "H," "Cet" must be used instead of "ce."

Ex.:
- cet homme -> ce vieil homme ; (This old man)
- cet artisan -> ce jeune artisan ; (This artisan)
- ce discours -> cet accablant discours. (This overwhelming speech)

Possessive determinants

The possessive determinant, unlike other determinants, indicates that a thing or a person belongs to another person or something else.

Ex.:
- Nous **te** confions notre chien.

 We entrust our dog to you.

- Connais-tu **ma** cousine?

 Do you know my cousin?

Possessor	1st Person singular	2nd Person singular	3rd Person singular	1st Person plural	2nd Person plural	3rd Person plural
Masculine singular	mon	Ton	Son	notre	votre	leur
Feminine singular	ma	Ta	Sa	notre	votre	leur
Plural	mes	Tes	Ses	nos	vos	leurs

Note: Mon, ton and son can precede a feminine noun or adjective beginning with a vowel or mute "h."

Ex.:
- J'ai reçu mon salaire. (Salaire= masculine)
- Marie est ton amie. (Amie=feminine)
- C'est son histoire. (Histoire=feminine)

When it is placed before a verb, it is not a possessive determinant but a pronoun, the plural of the pronoun "Lui."

Ex.:

Alain leur (= lui, pronoun) donne leurs (= (une) part, determinant) part

Exclamatory determinants

"*Que, Quel, quelle, quelles*" are the exclamative determinants that replace "What, Such" in English.

They change in gender and number.

Like all determinants, the exclamatory determinant changes according to the name it determines.

Ex.:

Quelle belle maison ! (Feminine singular)

Quels beaux vases !(Masculine plural)

Use:

The exclamatory determinants are used in direct or indirect exclamation sentences.

- Quelle robe ! (What a dress!)

- J'imagine quelle déception tu as dû ressentir. (I imagine the disappointment you must have felt.)

They are used in front of a verb of state. Placed before a verb of state, the exclamatory determinant is the attribute of the subject and then agrees with the name to which it is associated.

Ex.:

Quelle fut sa rage quand il vit l'état de sa maison!

What was his rage when he saw the condition of his house!

Interrogative determinants

"*Que, Quel, quelle, quelles*" are the interrogative determinants replacing "What" in English.

Just like the exclamative determinants, these change in gender and in number. They are placed before a conjugated verb and are used in interrogative sentences.

Ex.:

- QUELLE EST VOTRE FONCTION DANS CETTE ÉCOLE?
- QUELLES SONT VOS LOISIRS PRÉFÉRÉS ?

Indefinite determinants

They indicate an unencrypted quantity or a vague evocation of a person or thing.

There are several indefinite determinants.:

TOUT, AUCUN, CHAQUE, MAINT, NUL, PLUSIEURS, TEL, QUELQUES, DIVERS, DIFFÉRENT, CERTAIN (all, none, each, maint, null, several, such, some, various, different, certain)

BEAUCOUP DE, TROP DE, PLUS DE, SUFFISAMMENT DE, TANT DE (a lot of, too much, more, enough, so much)

Ex.:
- CHAQUE RÉPONSE DOIT ÊTRE JUSTIFIÉE PAR UNE EXPLICATION.
- JEANNE A PLUSIEURS POUPÉES.

- Each answer must be justified by an explanation.

- Jeanne has several dolls.

Cardinal numeral determinants

They are used to indicate the number of people or things.

Ex.:

J'ai **une** (1) amie

Elle a **sept (7)** ans

3.5 Direct object pronoun

A direct object pronoun replaces a noun that is the object of a sentence. The direct object pronouns in French are:

me (me)

te (you)

le (him/it)

la (her/it)

nous (us)

vous (you)

les (them)

The pronoun comes **before** all parts of the verb.

J'aime les légumes (I like vegetables.) --> Je **les** déteste (I hate them.)

Nous avons mangé les gâteaux de ta mère (We ate your mother's cakes.) --> Nous **les** avons entendu (We heard them)

If the verb is followed by a verb in the **infinitive**, the pronoun comes **before** the infinitive.

J'aime **la** regarder (I like to look at her.)

Nous allons **vous** attendre à la gare (We're going to wait for you at the train station.)

Before a vowel or a silent h, me changes to m', te changes to t', le and la change to l'.

Elle **m'**aime (She loves me.)

Je **t'**aime (I love you.)

Nous **l'**avons mangé (We ate it.)

CHAPTER 4 - CONJUGATION

4.1 Tenses

In French conjugation, we distinguish personal modes- the indicative, subjunctive and imperative modes that address a person, and impersonal modes- the gerondif, the participle, and the infinitive.

We have seen the three verb groups, so now we can conjugate according to their verbal group.

4.1.1 Indicative Mode:

The indicative mode is conjugated like the subjunctive and the imperative, which means in personal mode (who addresses directly to the subject or the person). An indicative mood is a verb form which makes a statement or asks a question. The vast majority of sentences are in the indicative mood. The terminations of conjugated verbs vary according to the group of verbs. The time frames of the indicative are as follows:

"Présent": describes something that happens in the present time; it can also be accompanied or supplemented with a complement

Complements indicating the present

Maintenant (Now) and et en ce moment (in this moment)

-**"Passé composé"** (compound past): describes an action that has already happened

-**"L'imparfait"** (the imperfect): similar to the compound past; the action has already happened, but can be reproduced

"Le plus-que-Parfait": the past of the "imparfait" or the "more-than perfect"; added to one of the two, it describes the anteriority of an action already past

Passé simple: tells a brief action that has already happened

Passé antérieur: is often used with the simple past to situate the prior art of an action already passed

Complements indicating the past: Hier (Yesterday)

Futur simple: describes a wish, a project that has not yet been realized

Futur antérieur: a time in the future that anticipates the future before the action that precedes this future is realized; it is often used in a single sentence before the simple future

Complements indicating the future: Demain (Tomorrow), Après (After)

Conjugation of the verbs of the first group

The verbs of the first group are "regular" verbs, except the verb "Aller" (To go). Their endings are all the same.

In the present, the terminations are as follows:

-e,-es,-e,-ons,-ez-, -ent.

Ex.:

Verb:Mang**ER** (To eat)

Je mang**e**	Nous mang**eons**
Tu mang**es**	Vous mang**ez**
Il/Elle mang**e**	Ils mang**ent**

In the passé compose, it is necessary to follow this formula.

OR

Pronouns	Auxiliary « avoir »	Auxiliary « être »	
j' / je	ai	Suis	
	+ as		+Past Participle
Tu		Es	
il / elle / on	A	Est	
Nous	avons	Sommes	

| Vous | avez | Etes |
| ils / elles | ont | Sont |

Which gives pronoun in blue (1), auxiliary "Avoir" or "Etre" in red (2), and past participle in black (3).

J'ai mang**é**

Tu as mang**é**

Il a mang**é**

Nous avons mang**é**

Vous avez mang**é**

Ils ont mang**é**

Another example with the verb Fatiguer (To be tired)

Je me suis fatigu**é**

Tu t'es fatigu**é**

Il s'est fatigu**é**

Nous nous sommes fatigu**és**

Vous vous êtes fatigu**és**

Ils se sont fatigu**és**

In the **imparfait**, terminations are: -eais,-eais,-eait,-ions,-iez-,-eaient.

Verb :MangWE (To eat)

Je mang**eais**

Tu mang**eais**

Il/Elle mang**eait**

Nous mang**ions**

Vous mang**iez**

Ils mang**eaient**

In the **plus-que-parfait**, the formula to follow is: Pronoun +auxilliary « Avoir » or « être » joint in the imparfait+ past participle

J'avais mang**é**

Tu avais mang**é**

Il avait mang**é**

Nous avions mang**é**

Vous aviez mang**é**

Ils avaient mang**é**

In the **passé simple**, terminations are: -eai,-eas,-ea,-iâmes,-âtes-,-érent

Je mang**eai**

Tu mang**eas**

Il mang**ea**

Nous mang**eâmes**

Vous mang**eâtes**

Ils mang**èrent**

In the **passé antérieur,** the formula is: Pronoun + auxiliary« Avoir » or« etre » in the passé simple tense+ past participle

J'eus mangé

Tu eus mangé

Il eut mangé

Nous eûmes mangé

Vous eûtes mangé

Ils eurent mangé

In the **futur simple**, terminations are: -erai,-eras,-era,-erons,-erez-,-eront

Futur simple

Je mang**erai**

Tu mang**eras**

Il mang**era**

Nous mang**erons**

Vous mang**erez**

Ils mang**eront**

In the futur antérieur, **the** formula is: pronoun + auxiliary « Avoir » or « etre » in the futur simple tense + past participle

J'aurai mang**é**

Tu auras mang**é**

Il aura mang**é**

Nous aurons mang**é**

Vous aurez mang**é**

Ils auront mang**é**

Conjugation of the verbs of the second group

The verbs of the second group are "regular" verbs ending with "-IR."

Ex.:

Verb: Finir (To end)

In the **présent**, the terminations are: -is,-is,-it,-issons, -issez-,-issent

Je fin**is**

Tu fin**is**

Il fin**it**

Nous fin**issons**

Vous fin**issez**

Ils fin**issent**

In the **passé composé** the formula is: pronoun + auxilliary « avoir » + past participle

J'ai fini

Tu as fini

Il a fini

Nous avons fini

Vous avez fini

Ils ont fini

In the **imparfait**, temrinations are: -issais, -issais,-issait,-issions, -issiez-,-issaient

Je finissais

Tu finissais

Il finissait

Nous finissions

Vous finissiez

Ils finissaient

In the **plus-que-parfait**, the formula is: Pronoun + aux « Avoir » orêtre » in the Imparfait's tense+ past participle

J'avais fin**i**
Tu avais fin**i**
Il avait fin**i**
Nous avions fin**i**

Vous aviez fini

Ils avaient fini

In the **passé simple**, terminations are: -is,-is,- it,-îmes, -îtes-,-irent

Je finis

Tu finis

Il finit

Nous finîmes

Vous finîtes

Ils finirent

In the **passé antérieur**,the formula is : pronoun + auxiliary« Avoir » or « etre » in the passé simple+ past participle

J'eus fini
Tu eus fini
Il eut fini
Nous eûmes fini
Vous eûtes fini
Ils eurent fini

In the **futur simple**, the terminations are : -irai, -iras,-ira,-irons,-irez-,-oront

Je finirai
Tu finiras
il finira
nous finirons
vous finirez
ils finiront

In the **futur antérieur,** the formula is: pronoun + auxiliary « avoir » or« etre » in the futur simple+ past participle

J'aurai fini
Tu auras fini
Il aura fini
Nous aurons fini
Vous aurez fini
Ils auront fini

Note: The terminations of the first group and the second group do not vary much for the personal pronouns **NOUS, VOUS, ILS.** Usually, they remain as *-ons, -ez, -ont.*

When should we use the auxiliary "Avoir" or "Etre" in the passé composé?

When the subject performs the action, the auxilliary "Avoir" is used.

Ex.:

Regarder la télévision (Watching TV)

Passé composé: J'**ai** regardé la télévision. (I watched TV.)

It is the subject who performs the action.

Action : Watching TV

On the other hand, when the subject undergoes the action, that is where the auxiliary "Etre" is used. It describes a state.

Ex.:

Etre fatigué (To be tired)

Passé compose: Je **suis** fatigué (I am tired.)

State: Fatigué (Tired)

Subject : Je

Practical exercise:

Conjugate the verbs of the first group at all the times of the indicative.

-Prier (To pray)

-Jouer (To play)

And the verbs of the second group:

-Partir (To go)

-Grandir (To grow)

We have seen the conjugation of the verbs called "regular".

Let us continue to the conjugation of the verbs of the third group.

Conjugation of the verbs of the third group

In the *present of the indicative*, most of the verbs of the 3rd group have the terminations:

-s -s -t -ons -ez –ent

Verbs ending with *-DRE,* such as vendre, perdre, coudre, end with:

-ds -ds -d -ons -ez –ent

Let's take as an example the verb Vendre (To sell):

Présent	Passé composé
Je vend**s**	J'ai vend**u**
Tu vend**s**	Tu as vend**u**
Il vend	Il a vend**u**
Nous vend**ons**	Nous avons vend**u**
Vous vend**ez**	Vous avez vend**u**
Ils vend**ent**	Ils ont vend**u**

Imparfait	Plus-que-parfait
Je vend**ais**	J'avais vend**u**
Tu vend**ais**	Tu avais vend**u**
Il vend**ait**	Il avait vend**u**
Nous vend**ions**	Nous avions vend**u**
Vous vend**iez**	Vous aviez vend**u**
Ils vend**aient**	Ils avaient vend**u**

Passé simple	Passé antérieur
Je vend**is**	J'eus vend**u**
Tu vend**is**	Tu eus vend**u**
Il vend**it**	Il eut vend**u**
Nous vend**îmes**	Nous eûmes vend**u**
Vous vend**îtes**	Vous eûtes vend**u**
Ils vend**irent**	Ils eurent vend**u**

Futur simple	Futur antérieur
Je vend**rai**	J'aurai vend**u**
Tu vend**ras**	Tu auras vend**u**
Il vend**ra**	Il aura vend**u**
Nous vend**rons**	Nous aurons vend**u**
Vous vend**rez**	Vous aurez vend**u**
Ils vend**ront**	Ils auront vend**u**

Except the verbs which end with *-aindre, -eindre, -oindre, -soudre* such as Craindre, Peindre, Joindre, Résoudre, which follow the general rule and end with

-s -s -t -ons -ez -ent

Let's take as an example the verb Peindre (To paint)

Présent	- Passé composé
Je peins	J'ai peint
Tu peins	Tu as peint
Il peint	Il a peint
Nous peignons	Nous avons peint
Vous peignez	Vous avez peint
Ils peignent	Ils ont peint

Imparfait	Plus-que-parfait
Je peignais	J'avais peint
Tu peignais	Tu avais peint
Il peignait	Il avait peint
Nous peignions	Nous avions peint
Vous peigniez	Vous aviez peint
Ils peignaient	Ils avaient peint

Passé simple	Passé antérieur
Je peignis	J'eus peint
Tu peignis	Tu eus peint
Il peignit	Il eut peint
Nous peignîmes	Nous eûmes peint
Vous peignîtes	Vous eûtes peint
Ils peignirent	Ils eurent peint

Futur simple	Futur antérieur
Je peindrai	J'aurai peint
Tu peindras	Tu auras peint
Il peindra	Il aura peint
Nous peindrons	Nous aurons peint
Vous peindrez	Vous aurez peint
Ils peindront	Ils auront peint

Pouvoir, Vouloir, Valoir's verbs end with :-*x -x -t -ons -ez –ent*

Verb: Vouloir (To want)

Présent	Passé composé
Je v**eux**	J'ai v**oulu**
Tu v**eux**	Tu as v**oulu**
Il v**eut**	Il a v**oulu**
Nous v**oulons**	Nous avons v**oulu**
Vous v**oulez**	Vous avez v**oulu**
Ils v**eulent**	ils ont v**oulu**

Imparfait	Plus-que-parfait
Je v**oulais**	J'avais v**oulu**
Tu v**oulais**	Tu avais v**oulu**
Il v**oulait**	Il avait v**oulu**
Nous v**oulions**	Nous avions v**oulu**
Vous v**ouliez**	Vous aviez v**oulu**
Ils v**oulaient**	Ils avaient v**oulu**

Passé simple	Passé antérieur
Je v**oulus**	J'eus v**oulu**
Tu v**oulus**	Tu eus v**oulu**
Il v**oulut**	Il eut v**oulu**
Nous v**oulûmes**	Nous eûmes v**oulu**
Vous v**oulûtes**	Vous eûtes v**oulu**
Ils v**oulurent**	Ils eurent v**oulu**

Futur simple	Futur antérieur
Je v**oudrai**	J'aurai v**oulu**
Tu v**oudras**	Tu auras v**oulu**
Il v**oudra**	Il aura v**oulu**
Nous v**oudrons**	Nous aurons v**oulu**
Vous v**oudrez**	Vous aurez v**oulu**
Ils v**oudront**	Ils auront v**oulu**

The verbs "Ouvrir"and "Cueillir" end in the present just as the verbs of the first group.

-e -es -e -ons -ez –ent

Note: The past participles of the verbs of the first group, the second group, and the third group are as follows:

Radical + termination é for the verbs of the first and second group and for those of the second group

Ex. 1: Parler (Verb ending with –er, verb of the first group)

Radical : Parl+**é**

Past Participle : Parl**é**

Ex. 2 : Partir (Verb ending with –ir, verb of the second group)

Radical : Part+**i**

Past Participle : Part**i**

Ex. 3 : Valoir (Verb ending with –oir, verb of the third group)

Radical : Val+**oir**

Past Participle : Val**u**

Now, let's conjugate the verbs: "Etre", "Avoir", "Dire", which are the most frequently used verbs.

Conjugation of the verb Etre :

Présent	Imparfait
Je **suis**	J'**étais**
Tu **es**	Tu **étais**
Il/Elle **est**	Il/Elle **était**
Nous **sommes**	Nous **étions**
Vous **êtes**	Vous **étiez**
Ils **sont**	Ils **étaient**
Passé simple	**Passé composé**
Je **fus**	J'ai **été**
Tu **fus**	Tu as **été**
Il/Elle **fut**	Il a **été**
Nous **fûmes**	Nous avons **été**
Vous **fûtes**	Vous avez **été**
Ils **furent**	Ils ont **été**
The simple past is used when the action happened a long time ago.	

Futur simple	
Je **serai**	The compound past is usually used to tell a story already passed, or to the indirect speech.
Tu **seras**	
Il **sera**	The simple future describes the near future, an action that will happen.
Nous **serons**	
Vous **serez**	
Ils **seront**	

Conjugation of the Verb Avoir :

Présent	Passé composé
J'**ai**	J'ai **eu**
Tu **as**	Tu as **eu**
Il **a**	Il a **eu**
Nous **avons**	Nous avons **eu**
Vous **avez**	Vous avez **eu**
Ils **ont**	Ils ont **eu**

Imparfait	Passé simple
J'**avais**	J'**eus**
Tu **avais**	Tu **eus**
Il **avait**	Il **eut**
Nous **avions**	Nous **eûmes**
Vous **aviez**	Vous **eûtes**
Ils **avaient**	Ils **eurent**

Futur simple	
J'**aurai**	
Tu **auras**	
Il **aura**	
Nous **aurons**	
Vous **aurez**	
Ils **auront**	

Conjugation of the Verb Dire:

Présent	Imparfait
Je d**is**	Je d**isais**
Tu d**is**	Tu d**isais**
Il d**it**	Il d**isait**
Nous d**isons**	Nous d**isions**
Vous d**ites**	Vous d**isiez**
Ils d**isent**	Ils d**isaient**

Passé composé	Passé simple
J'ai d**it**	Je d**is**
Tu as d**it**	Tu d**is**
Il a d**it**	Il d**it**
Nous avons d**it**	Nous d**îmes**
Vous avez d**it**	Vous d**îtes**
Ils ont d**it**	Ils dir**ent**

Futur simple	
Je d**irai**	
Tu d**iras**	
Il d**ira**	
Nous d**irons**	
Vous d**irez**	
Ils d**iront**	

4.1.2 The conditional mode

Conditional mode expresses a wish or a project, but under conditions or doubts.

It combines only with the present and the past.

At present

Termination of the verbs of the first group:

We just conjugate the verb to the future de l'indicatif with the endings of the imparfait.

Terminations of the verbs of the first group with the verb "Aimer":

Je -**erais** (J'aimerais)

Tu –**erais** (Tu aimerais)

Il **–erait** (Il aimerait)

Nous **–erions** (Nous aimerions)

Vous **–eriez** (Vous aimeriez)

Ils **–eraient** (Ils aimeraient)

And for the other groups, it would be:

-rais

-rais

-rait

-rions

-riez

-raient

Ex. with Finir

Je finirais

Tu finirais

Il finirait

Nous finirions

Vous finiriez

Ils finiraient

Terminations of the verbs of the third group are as follows:

-drais
-drais
-drait
-drions
_driez
-draient

<u>Conditional</u> **(Verb"Vouloir")**

The Conditional is conjugated only into the present and the past.

Présent	**Passé**
Je v**oudrais**	J'aurais v**oulu**
Tu v**oudrais**	Tu aurais v**oulu**
Il v**oudrait**	Il aurait v**oulu**
Nous v**oudrions**	Nous aurions v**oulu**
Vous v**oudriez**	Vous auriez v**oulu**
Ils v**oudraient**	Ils auraient v**oulu**

4.1.3 Subjunctive mode

To conjugate to the subjunctive, it is sufficient to add "que" or "qu" before the verb conjugated to the present or the past. The future does not conjugate with the subjunctive

Ex.:

Que nous mangions ; que vous mangiez …

Qu'il soit ; qu'ils viennent… (Que= That)

CHAPTER 5- TYPES OF SENTENCES

On our path to building a sentence, we have studied the personal pronouns subject, the conjugated verbs that go with it, and complements. Naturally, we have to start at the beginning with basic French sentence structure. Like English, French is an SVO, or Subject-Verb-Object, language. The French language does not drop the subject in most cases. In order to build even the simplest French sentence, you will need two or three elements. There are three types of sentences.

5.1 Simple sentences

The simple sentence is also called an independent proposition because it is not related to any other sentence. It is autonomous.

Among the simple sentences, there are two different kinds, verbal phrases and nominal sentences.

The verbal phrase

A verbal phrase is composed of a nominal group (personal subject pronouns or names) and a verbal group, followed by one or more complements, though not all simple sentences contain complements. The complement does not belong to the subject nominal group or to the verbal group. It can be moved to the beginning or the end of the sentence.

Ex.:

Anne marche toute seule (Anne walks alone.)

La table est prête pour le dîner (The table is ready for dinner.)

Ce soir, nous sortons en boîte (Tonight, we go on a night club.)

La pluie tombe (The rain falls.)

L'enfant pleure (The kid cries.)

If a sentence uses an intransitive verb, it will be a SV sentence:

Je suis. *(*I am.)

Je in this sentence is the subject, and *suis* is the intransitive verb. Since intransitive verbs do not need to take objects (verbs like *aller* (to go), *courir* (to run), *sauter* (to jump) or danser (to dance)), there is no O in this sentence. This is one of the simplest French sentences you can build.

Nominal sentence

As the name implies, the nominal sentence is a sentence without a verb, only names.

Ex.:

Premier essai, premier échec (First try, first failure)

Besoin d'argent, besoin de travail (Needing money, needing job)

5.2 Compound sentences

The compound sentence consists of two independent propositions, coordinated or juxtaposed, and therefore contains two conjugated verbs.

Two Coordinated Proposals

When the sentence is composed of two coordinated propositions, it suffices to add a conjunction of coordination to connect the two propositions.

Coordinating conjunction list:

Mais, ou, et, donc, or ,ni, car

Coordinating conjunction:

This marks the union: Et

Ex.:

Ce repas est délicieux **et** bien préparé

(This meal is delicious and well prepared.)

This marks the opposition: Mais, pourtant

Ex.:

Ce repas est délicieux **mais** je n'ai plus faim

(This meal is delicious, but I am no longer hungry.)

This marks the alternative or the negation: Ni, ou

Ex.:

Ce repas est délicieux ou c'est moi qui ai faim ? (This meal is delicious, or is it me who's hungry?)

This marks the consequence: Donc

Ex.:

Ce repas est délicieux donc je veux en reprendre

(This meal is delicious, so I want to take more.)

This marks the conclusion: Donc

Ex.:

Ce plat est appétissant mais je n'ai plus faim.

(This dish is appetizing, but I am no longer hungry.)

Coordinating conjunction list:

but	Mais
or	Ou
and	Et
thus	Donc
neither a nor b	ni a ni b
because	Car
Addition	
besides	d'ailleurs
furthermore	en outre, de plus
moreover	de plus
what is more	que plus est, bien plus
by the way	soit dit en passant
in addition	de surcroit, en outre
in fact	en fait
in other words	en d'autres termes
that is to say	c'est-à-dire

so that	afin que
so as to [+verb]	pour que [+ verbe]
in order to	afin de
for	pour
to this end	à cet effet
Cause	
because	parce que
because of	en raison de
as	comme
for	car
thanks to	grâce à
due to	du au fait que
on account of	étant donné que
given that	étant donné que
Comparaison	
as though	comme si
as if	comme si
in comparison	par comparaison
Concession	
although	bien que
though	bien que
even though	même si
in spite of	Malgré
despite	Malgré

all the same	malgré tout

Contrast and Opposition

instead of	au lieu de
nevertheless	néanmoins, toutefois
notwithstanding	nonobstant, néanmoins
otherwise	sinon, autrement
else	Sinon
whereas	tandis, alors que
yet	cependant, pourtant
conversely	inversement
however	cependant, toutefois
by contrast	par opposition

Restriction

as far as	dans la mesure de
as long as	du moment où

Condition

provided	à condition que
unless	à moins que
as long as	du moment que, à condition que
otherwise	sinon, autrement
then	alors

Consequence

so that	de telle sorte que
so much that	à tel point que
consequently	en conséquence

as a result	en conséquence
therefore	par conséquent
that is why	c'est pourquoi
this is because	c'est parce que, la raison en est que
thus	ainsi
hence	d'où

Two juxtaposed proposals

When the sentence is composed of two juxtaposed propositions, we use a punctuation mark between the propositions.

Ex.:

Nous étions camarades de classe au lycée, nous nous appelons encore de temps en temps.

We were classmates at high school; we still call each others from time to time.

5.3 Complex sentences:

The complex sentence is composed of several conjugated verbs. It contains a main proposal, followed or accompanied by one or more subordinate proposals. It is often related to the subordinate proposition by a relative pronoun.

Relative pronouns

Relative pronouns replace the subject or object that precedes it. It varies in kind and in number; however, most of them are invariable.

Invariable relative pronouns

qui - que - quoi - dont - où

Qui: (That, Who)

"Qui" has a double meaning. "Qui" replaces an object (table, chair etc.) and also a person or an animal. In English, it has several variants, depending on the circumstances (that,who) and the subject, but not in French.

Ex.:

L'homme qui est venu me chercher est mon père. (People)

(The man who came to fetch me is my father.)

Le chien qui aboie *fait peur (Animals)*

*(*The dog who's barking is scary.*)*

Le bus qui doit me prendre est en retard (Things, not alive)

*(*The bus that has to take me is late.*)*

Que: (That)

The relative pronoun "Qui" has a subject function; that is, it replaces the preceding subject. The relative pronoun "Que" has a complement function; it replaces the complement that precedes it.

Ex.:

la fille **qui** est à côté de moi est très jolie

« **Qui** » replaces la fille . la fille est jolie (The girl is pretty.)

Le livre **que** tu me donnes semble trop vieux

"Que" replaces the word "livre," which is a complement. (You give me the book which is too old.*)*

Let's take the example we used above.

" Le bus qui doit me prendre est en retard" *(*The bus that has to take me is late*)* would become, "Le bus que je dois prendre est en retard*"* *(*The bus I have to take is late*)*.

Subject: Le bu, because the bus is late.

In two sentences it would be:

Le bus est en retard. Je dois prendre ce bus.

The bus is late. I have to take this bus.

Quoi : (What)

This is only used when you talk about things or objects. It is just a complement in a sentence.

Ex.:

Je ne sais pas quoi penser de cette société

I do not know what to think of this society.

Dont: (Of which)

The relative pronoun "Dont" may have different functions. It replaces people, animals or things.

Cette belle maison dont je t'ai parlé est à vendre. *(This beautiful house of which I spoke to you is for sale.)*

Here is "complement of direct object" indirect object. (I told you about this pretty house.)

Voici le professeur dont les cours sont captivants. (Les cours de ce professeur sont captivants)

Here is the teacher whose courses are captivating. (This teacher's courses are captivating.)

Où: (Where)

The relative pronoun "Où" is also called a circumstantial complement of place or time.

Place : Cette ville est l'endroit où j'ai grandi

J'ai grandi dans cette ville

This city is where I grew up

I grew up in this city

Time : Je me souviens de l'époque où je passais mes vacances chez mes grands parents

Je passais mes vacances chez mes grands parents à l'époque

I remember the time when I spent my holidays with my grandparents.

I spent my holidays with my grandparents at the time.

5.4 The different forms of phrases

5.4.1 The affirmative sentence

We have already seen quite a number of affirmative sentences in previous courses. The affirmative sentence affirms something.

Ex.:

Je cherche mon train

I'm looking for my train.

Ils sont là

They are there.

Nous te cherchions

We were looking for you.

Les chiens aboient

Dogs bark.

5.4.2 The negative sentence

To mark the negation, the French language uses this formula:

Subject + **ne** + verb + **pas** + complement.

Ex.:

Affirmative: Je cherche mon train

Negative: Je ne cherche pas mon train

Nous te cherchions

Nous ne te cherchions pas

Les chiens aboient

Les chiens n'aboient pas

Ne…pas mark the negation.

Another word that marks the negation is "Jamais."

"Jamais" marks the negation on an uncontrollable scale because it is used for a wish that will not change, or an action without appeal. Do not add "Pas" when using "Jamais."

Affirmative: Les chiens aboient

Negative: Les chiens n'aboient pas

Negative using Jamais: Les chiens n'aboient jamais

5.4.3 The exclamatory sentence

The exclamatory sentence is marked by the presence of an exclamation mark at the end. It expresses surprise, astonishment, anger.

Ex.:

Quel temps horrible !

Quelle petite peste cette fille !Quelle audace il a eu de me répondre en classe Quelle belle journée !

What a horrible timeWhat a small plague this girl!

What daring he had to answer me in class!

Such a good day!

5.4.4 The interrogative sentence

The interrogative sentence is used to ask a question. It is marked by a "?" at the end of the sentence.

Unlike other types of sentence, what characterizes the interrogative sentence is the disposition of the elements in it.

Declarative sentence	Interrogative sentence	Formula
Tu cherches ton chemin (Your search your way)	Cherches-tu ton chemin? Est-ce-que tu cherches ton chemin?	Verb+ Personal pronoun subject +Complement+ ? Est-ce-que+Personal pronoun subject +complement+ ?
Vous connaissez le chemin pour aller à l'école (You know the way to go to school.)	Connaissez-vous le chemin pour aller à l'école? Est-ce-que vous connaissez le chemin pour aller à l'école ?	Verb+ Personal pronoun subject +Complements+ ? Est-ce-que+ Personal pronoun subject +complement+ ?

It is also possible to ask a question by putting an adverb or an interrogative pronoun at the beginning of the sentence.

The formula Verb + Subject + Complement +? does not change.

Inversion Questions in French

One of the easiest sorts of questions to ask in French is called an inversion question. It is named so because of the way in which the question is formed, by inverting the subject and the verb of the sentence and just adding a "?" at the end.

As-tu un chat ?

Do you have a cat?

If you want to ask an even wider variety of questions, you can use French question words alongside the *est-ce que* structure. French question words include **qui** (who), **quand** (when), **où** (where), **pourquoi** (why) and **comment** (how). These words are simply tacked on to the beginning of an **est-ce que** question in order to have the desired meaning.

Qui est-ce que tu cherches ?

Who are you searching?

Quand est-ce qu'on atterit?

When are we landing?

Où est-ce qu'on va ?

Where are we going?

Pourquoi est-ce que tu cries?

Why are you screaming?

Comment est-ce que ça marche ?

How does it work?

Que :

Que fais-tu ? (What do you do ?)

Que vas-tu faire? (What are you going to do ?)

Qui: "Qui" is used to ask a question about a person.

Ex.:

Qui est là ? (Who's there?)

Qui va venir à ma fête demain ? (Who's coming to my party tomorrow?)

Qui veux-tu que j'appelle aussi tard ? (Who do you want me to call this late?)

Quand:

"Quand" is used to know the time.

Ex.:

Quand est-ce-que tu arrive à Paris ?

Quand pourrais-je passer chez toi ?

When do you come to Paris?

When can I go to you?

Quoi / De quoi / À quoi :

These are used in a question to know the details, and to talk about a thing or a situation.

Ex.:

A quoi penses-tu ?

De quoi as-tu peur ?

Maintenant, je fais quoi ?

What are you thinking about?

What are you afraid of?

Now what do I do?

<u>Où:</u>

"Où" is used to ask about a place.

Ex.:

Où est-ce-que tu habites?

Où allons-nous dormir ?

Où se trouve ma serviette ?

Where do you live?

Where are we going to sleep?

Where is my towel?

That being said, there are two types of questions:

The total query:

The total query is a question whose answers are either "Oui" or "Non."

Ex.:

As-tu faim ? (*Are you hungry*?)

-Non (*No*)

Or

-Non, je n'ai pas faim. (*No, I'm not*)

Veux-tu que je t'aide ? (*Do you want me to help you* ?)

-Oui (*Yes*)

Question Tags in French: *Est-ce que* (and *Qu'est-ce que*)

The basic question tag in French is **"*Est-ce que*."** It marks the beginning of a yes/no question, much in the same way that inversion does. ***The difference here is that the sentence that follows will retain the basic French sentence structure.***

Est-ce que tu veux partir ? — Do you want to leave?

Qu'est-ce que is a variation on this question tag. By putting que or "what" at the beginning, you can ask a question requiring a more elaborate answer (The Partial query).

Qu'est-ce que tu veux manger ? — What do you want to eat?

The partial query

The partial query concerns one of the elements of the sentence; it can not be answered with "Oui" or "Non."

The answers are often explanations for the answer given.

Ex.:

Pourquoi ne veux-tu pas répondre ?

-Parce que je n'en ai pas envie.

Où est-ce-que tu habite ?

-J'habite aux alentours de Marseille.

Why don't you want to answer?

-Because I do not feel like it.

Where do you live?

-I live in the neighborhoods of Marseille.

The imperative or injunctive sentence

The imperative phrase, from the word "imperative," gives orders, counsel, or prohibits something. It ends with a point or an exclamation point. It may include a subject or not. It indicates that the speaker desires for the action expressed in the sentence to take place. In most imperative sentences, there's an implied *you*.

Ex.:

Arrête de parler (Stop talking.)

Je te dis d'arrêter de parler (I tell you to stop talking.)

Je veux que tu arrête de parler ! (I want you to stop talking!)

5.4.5 Polite phrases:

French speakers use the subject "Vous" for politeness.

"Bonjour" (Good morning) and "Merci" (Thank you) are the most used terms in French for politeness.

To ask a question (to strangers or old people or just someone you don't personally know) in a formal and polite way, you have to use this formula:

Bonjour + est-ce-que+ question+ s'il-vous-plaît ?

Ex.:

Bonjour, est-ce-que vous pouvez m'aider s'il-vous-plaît ?

Hello, can you help me please?

"S'il-vous-plaît" (Plural and mostly used for polite or formal conversation) and "S'il-te-plaît' (Singular, less formal but is fine for young people talking to each other.)

CHAPTER 6 - EXPRESSIONS

6.1 Language

Do you speak French?	Parlez-vous français?
Yes, I speak French.	Oui, je parle français.
What did you say?	Qu'est-ce que vous avez dit?
I don't understand.	Je ne vous comprends pas.
Please say that again.	Dites-le encore, s'il-vous-plaît.
Can you repeat that, please?	Vous pouvez répéter s'il-vous-plaît ?
Could you speak more slowly, please?	Est-ce que vous pouvez parler plus lentement, s'il-vous-plaît?
Please speak slowly.	Parlez plus lentement, s'il-vous-plaît.
What is this called?	Comment on appelle ça?
What is this in English?	Comment dit on en anglais?
How do you say that in English?	Comment ça se dit en anglais?
How do you spell it?	Comment ça s'écrit ?

Finding Your Way

Where is the station / next bus-station / city center?	Où est la gare / station de bus / centre-ville?

Where can I get a newspaper?	Où puis-je trouver un journal?
Where can I find a toilet?	Où puis-je trouver des toilettes?
Where can I buy some stamps?	Où puis-je acheter des timbres?
Is there a toilet near here?	Y a-t-il des toilettes près d'ici?
How far is it?	C'est à quelle distance?
How far is it to the city center / to the next bus station?	A quelle distance est le centre-ville / la station de bus la plus proche.
Not far from here.	Pas loin d'ici.
on the left	sur la gauche
on the right	sur la droite
straight ahead	tout droit
When does the bus leave?	Quand part le bus?
Your bus left an hour ago.	Votre bus est parti il y a une heure.
What time is breakfast / lunch / dinner?	A quelle heure est le petit-déjeuner / déjeuner / dîner?
Would you wake me tomorrow morning at 8 o'clock, please.	Est-ce que vous pouvez me réveiller demain à 8 heures, s'il-vous-plaît.
Your passport, please.	Votre passeport, s'il-vous-plaît.

6.2 Essential and basics

English	French
Hello	Bonjour
Good evening	Bonsoir
Goodbye	Au revoir
See you later	A plus tard
Yes	Oui
No	Non
Excuse me!	S'il vous plait
Thanks	Merci
Thanks a lot	Merci beaucoup !
Thank you for your help	Merci pour votre aide
Don't mention it	Je vous en prie
Ok	D'accord
How much is it please?	Quel est le prix s'il vous plaît ?
Sorry!	Pardon !
I don't understand.	Je ne comprends pas
I get it.	J'ai compris
I don't know.	Je ne sais pas
Forbidden	Interdit

English	French
English	**French**
Excuse me, where are the toilets?	Où sont les toilettes s'il vous plaît ?
Happy New Year!	Bonne année !
Happy birthday!	Bon anniversaire !
Happy holiday!	Joyeuses fêtes !
Congratulations!	Félicitations !

Hello	Bonjour
Goodbye	Au revoir
Good morning	Bonjour (le matin)
Good afternoon	Bonjour (après-midi)
Good evening	Bonsoir
Thank you (very much).	Merci (beaucoup).
No, thank you.	Non merci.
Yes / No	Si, oui / Non
Please	S'il-vous-plaît.
Excuse me.	Excusez-moi.
I'm sorry.	Je suis désolé(e).
You're welcome.	Il n'y a pas de quoi.
Really?	Ah bon? C'est vrai?
I'd like ...	Je voudrais ...
Where is ... ? / Where are ... ?	Où est ... ? / Où sont ... ?
How ... ?	Comment ... ?

| Why ... ? | Pourquoi ... ? |
| When ... ? | Quand ... ? |

6.3 Conversation

English	**French**
Hello. How are you?	Bonjour. Comment vas-tu ?
Hello. I'm fine, thank you.	Bonjour. Ça va bien merci
Do you speak French?	Est-ce que tu parles français ?
No, I don't speak French.	Non, je ne parle pas français
Only a little bit	Seulement un petit peu
Where do you come from?	De quel pays viens-tu ?
What is your nationality?	Quelle est ta nationalité ?
I am English.	Je suis anglaise
And you, do you live here?	Et toi, tu vis ici ?
Yes, I live here.	Oui, j'habite ici
My name is Sarah, what's your name?	Je m'appelle Sarah, et toi ?
Julian	Julien
What are you doing here?	Qu'est-ce que tu fais ici ?
I am on holiday.	Je suis en vacances
We are on holiday.	Nous sommes en vacances
I am on a business trip.	Je suis en voyage d'affaire
I work here.	Je travaille ici

English	French
We work here.	Nous travaillons ici
Where are the good places to go out and eat?	Quels sont les bons endroits pour manger ?
Is there a museum in the neighbourhood?	Est-ce qu'il y a un musée à côté d'ici ?
Where could I get an internet connection?	Où est-ce que je pourrais me connecter à Internet ?

6.4 Looking for someone

English	French
Excuse me, is Sarah here?	Est-ce que Sarah est là s'il vous plaît ?
Yes, she's here.	Oui, elle est ici
She's out.	Elle est sortie
You can call her on her mobile phone.	Vous pouvez l'appeler sur son mobile
Do you know where I could find her?	Savez-vous où je pourrais la trouver ?
She is at work.	Elle est à son travail
She is at home.	Elle est chez elle
Excuse me, is Julien here?	Est-ce que Julien est là s'il vous plaît ?
Yes, he's here.	Oui, il est ici
He's out.	Il est sorti
Do you know where I could find him?	Savez-vous où je pourrais le trouver ?
You can call him on his mobile phone.	Vous pouvez l'appeler sur son mobile
He is at work.	Il est à son travail

English	French
He is at home.	Il est chez lui

6.5 The beach

English	French
The beach	La plage
Do you know where I can buy a ball?	Savez-vous où je peux acheter un ballon ?
There is a store in this direction.	Il y a une boutique dans cette direction
A ball	Un ballon
Binoculars	Des jumelles
A cap	Une casquette
A towel	Serviette
Sandals	Des sandales
A bucket	Seau
Suntan lotion	Crème solaire
Swimming trunks	Caleçon de bain
Sunglasses	Lunettes de soleil
Shellfish	Crustacé
Sunbathing	Prendre un bain de soleil
Sunny	Ensoleillé
Sunset	Coucher du soleil
Parasol	Parasol
Sunshine	Lever de Soleil
Sunstroke	Insolation

English	French
Is it dangerous to swim here?	Est-il dangereux de nager ici ?
No, it is not dangerous.	Non, ce n'est pas dangereux
Yes, it is forbidden to swim here.	Oui, c'est interdit de se baigner ici
Swim	Nager
Swimming	Natation
Wave	Vague
Sea	Mer
Dune	Dune
Sand	Sable
What is the weather forecast for tomorrow?	Quel temps fera-t-il demain ?
The weather is going to change.	Le temps va changer
It is going to rain.	Il va pleuvoir
It will be sunny.	Il va y avoir du soleil
It will be very windy.	Il y aura beaucoup de vent
Swimming suit	Maillot de bain
Sunshade	Ombre

6.6 Feelings

English	French
I really like your country.	J'aime beaucoup ton pays
I love you.	Je t'aime
I am happy.	Je suis heureux
I am sad.	Je suis triste
I feel great here.	Je me sens bien ici
I am cold.	J'ai froid
I am hot.	J'ai chaud
It's too big.	C'est trop grand
It's too small.	C'est trop petit
It's perfect.	C'est parfait
Do you want to go out tonight?	Est-ce que tu veux sortir ce soir ?
I would like to go out tonight.	J'aimerais sortir ce soir
It is a good idea.	C'est une bonne idée
I want to have fun.	J'ai envie de m'amuser
It is not a good idea.	Ce n'est pas une bonne idée
I don't want to go out tonight.	Je n'ai pas envie de sortir ce soir
I want to rest.	J'ai envie de me reposer
Would you like to do some sport?	Est-ce que tu veux faire du sport ?
Yes, I need to relax.	Oui, j'ai besoin de me défouler !

English	French
I play tennis.	Je joue au tennis
No thanks. I am tired already.	Non merci, je suis assez fatigue

6.7 Understanding

English	French
I don't understand.	Je ne comprends pas
Can you repeat please?	Tu peux répéter s'il te plaît ?
Can you talk a bit more slowly, please?	Est-ce que tu peux parler un peu plus lentement, s'il te plaît ?
Could you write it down, please?	Pourrais-tu l'écrire, s'il te plaît ?
I get it.	J'ai compris

6.8 Colours

English	French
I like the color of this table.	J'aime bien la couleur de cette table
It's red.	C'est du rouge
Blue	Bleu
Yellow	Jaune
White	Blanc
Black	Noir
Green	Vert
Orange	Orange

English	French
Purple	Violet
Grey	Gris

6.9 In case of trouble

English	French
Can you help me, please?	Pouvez-vous m'aider s'il vous plaît ?
I'm lost.	Je suis perdu
What would you like?	Que désirez-vous ?
What happened?	Que s'est-il passé ?
Where could I find an interpreter?	Où puis-je trouver un interprète ?
Where is the nearest chemist's shop?	Où se trouve la pharmacie la plus proche ?
Can you call a doctor, please?	Pouvez-vous appeler un médecin, s'il vous plaît ?
Which kind of treatment are you undergoing at the moment?	Quel traitement suivez-vous en ce moment ?
A hospital	Un hôpital
A chemist's	Une Pharmacie
A doctor	Un docteur
Medical department	Service médical
I lost my papers.	J'ai perdu mes papiers
My papers have been stolen.	Je me suis fait voler mes papiers

English	French
Lost-property office	Bureau des objets trouvés
First-aid station	Poste de secours
Emergency exit	Sortie de secours
The police	La Police
Papers	Papiers
Money	Argent
Passport	Passeport
Luggage	Bagages
I'm ok, thanks.	C'est bon, non merci
Leave me alone!	Laissez-moi tranquille !
Go away!	Partez !

6.10 Partying

English	French
It's late, I have to go!	Il est tard ! Je dois y aller !
Shall we meet again?	Pourrait-on se revoir ?
Yes, with pleasure.	Oui , avec plaisir
This is my address.	J'habite à cette adresse
Do you have a phone number?	Est-ce que tu as un numéro de téléphone ?
Yes, here you go.	Oui, le voilà

English	French
I had a lovely time.	J'ai passé un bon moment avec toi
Me too, it was a pleasure to meet you.	Moi aussi, ça m'a fait plaisir de faire ta connaissance
We will see each other soon.	Nous nous reverrons bientôt
I hope so too.	Je l'espère aussi
Goodbye	Au revoir !
See you tomorrow.	A demain
Bye!	Salut !

6.11 Bar

English	French
The bar	Le bar
Would you like to have a drink?	Tu veux boire quelque chose ?
To drink	Boire
Glass	Verre
With pleasure	Avec plaisir
What would you like?	Qu'est-ce que tu prends ?
What's on offer?	Qu'est-ce qu'il y a à boire ?
There is water or fruit juices.	Il y a de l'eau ou des jus de fruits
Water	Eau
Can you add some ice cubes, please?	Pouvez-vous ajouter des glaçons s'il vous plaît ?
Ice cubes	Des glaçons

English	French
Chocolate	Du chocolat
Milk	Du lait
Tea	Du thé
Coffee	Du café
With sugar	Avec du sucre
With cream	Avec de la crème
Wine	Du vin
Beer	De la bière
A tea please	Un thé s'il te plaît
A beer please	Une bière s'il te plaît
Tea	Du thé
Coffee	Du café
With sugar	Avec du sucre
With cream	Avec de la crème
Wine	Du vin
Beer	De la bière
A tea please	Un thé s'il te plaît
A beer please	Une bière s'il te plaît
What would you like to drink?	Qu'est-ce que vous voulez boire ?
Two teas please!	Deux thés s'il vous plaît !

English	French
Two beers please!	Deux bières s'il vous plait
Nothing, thanks	Rien, merci
Cheers!	Santé !
Can we have the bill please?	L'addition s'il vous plaît !

6.12 Family

English	French
Do you have family here?	Est-ce que tu as de la famille ici ?
My father	Mon père
My mother	Ma mere
My son	Mon fils
My daughter	Ma fille
A brother	Un frère
My boyfriend	Mon ami
My girlfriend	Mon amie
My husband	Mon mari
My wife	Ma femme

CHAPTER 7 –FRENCH VOCABULARY FOR TRAVEL AND VACATION

7.1 Airport and plane travel

to	land	Atterrir
to	take off	Décoller
	arrival	Arrive
	boarding	Embarquement
the departure		départ
	departures	Departs
a	flight	un vol
to	travel	Voyager
to	stop over	faire escale
to	fly	Voler
the gate		Porte
the control tower		tour de contrôle
the destination		Destination
a	flight number	numéro de vol
a	passenger	Passage
an	international flight	vol international

an airline	companie aérienne
the terminal	Aérogare
an airport	l'aéroport
the runway	la piste (d'atterrissage, de décollage)
a connecting flight	Correspondence
the duty-free shop	boutique hors taxes
a departure lounge	salle de depart

Formalities & Booking - Formalités

a Passport	un passeport
first class	première classe
business class	classe affaire
economy class	classe économique
a one-way (ticket)	(billet) aller simple
return ticket	(billet) aller-retour
checkin	l'enregistrement
to check in	enregistrer ses bagages
check-in desk	comptoir d'enregistrement
to declare	déclarer
the customs	la douane
boarding card	carte d'embarquement
to book	réserver

Baggage - baggages

baggage reclaim	retrait des bagages, réception des bagages
backpack	sac à dos

excess baggage	excédent de bagages
luggage, baggage	bagage
a bag	un sac
hand luggage	bagage à main
carry-on (US)	
flight (on the airplane)	vol (dans l'avion)
the crew	l'équipage
aisle seat	siège côté couloir
window seat	siège côté hublot
aisle	couloir, allée
cockpit	cockpit
exit	Sortie
cabin	cabine
pilot	pilote
seat	siège
emergency landing	atterrissage forcé
security checks	contrôle de sécurité
air steward /air stewardess	hôtesse de l'air, steward
seatbelt	ceinture
jet lag	Décalage horaire
first aid kit	trousse de premiers secours

7.2 Transport by train and train station

At the train station

train station	gare
platform	quai
station hall	hall de gare
waiting room	salle d'attente
the ticket office	le guichet
ticket machine	billetterie automatique, distributeur de titres de transport
(train) fare	tarif (de train)
ticket	un billet
a single ticket	un aller simple
a return ticket	un aller-retour
timetable	horaire, tableau des horaires
season ticket	carte d'abonnement
railcard	carte de chemin de fer
young person's railcard	une carte jeune
luggage	les bagages
left-luggage office	la consigne
Left-luggage locker	la consigne automatique
a (luggage) trolley	le chariot à bagages
the station master	le chef de gare
information desk	bureau des renseignements, accueil

Railway

track	voie ferrée

railway line — ligne de chemin de fer

express train — train express

fast train — train rapide

live rail — voie électrifiée

level crossing — passage à niveau

derailment — déraillement

train trip - voyage en train

first class — première classe

second class — deuxième classe

a passenger — un voyageur

train driver — conducteur de train

Conductor — contrôleur

ticket inspector — contrôleur

train crash — accident de train

seat — siège

seat number — numéro de siège

correspondance — connection

penalty fare — amende

to travel — voyager

to get on the train — monter dans le train

to get off the train — descendre du train

to punch (a ticket) — composter (un billet)

Useful phrases

Where is the railway station?   Où est la gare?

Where can I buy a ticket?	Où puis-je acheter un billet?
A single (return) to London please.	Je voudrais un aller simple (un aller-retour) pour Londres svp.
When does the next train for London leave?	A quelle heure part le prochain train pour Londres?
Where can I find a toilet?	Où puis-je trouver des toilettes?
Where can I get a taxi?	Où puis-je prendre un taxi?
How far is it?	C'est à quelle distance?

7.3 Boat trip

anchorage	mouillage
berth	couchette
boarding	embarquement
bridge	passerelle, poste de pilotage
cabin, stateroom	cabine
cabin with balcony	cabine balcon
chief engineer	le chef machine
chief purser	le commissaire principal
chief radio	le chef radio
courtesy flag	pavillon de courtoisie
crew, staff	équipage
cruise	croisière
deck	pont
dinghy	canot
disturbance	perturbation

	dock, pier	quai
	docked	posté à quai
	draft	tirant d'eau
	flag	pavillon
	foredeck	avant-pont
	gangway	passerelle
	gross registered tonnage	jauge brute
	harbour, port	port
	head officers	etat-major
	high water	pleine mer
	horn	corne
	jetty, pier	jetée
	knot speed	vitesse exprimée en noeuds
	Life-boat drill	exercice de sécurité
	life buoy	bouée de sauvetage
	lifejacket	gilet de sauvetage
	lighthouse	phare
	liner	paquebot
	log (book)	journal de bord
	muster station	point de rassemblement
	No-view cabin	cabine intérieure
	Outside-view cabin	cabine vue extérieure
	passageway	coursive
to	pitch	tanguer
	port of call	escale

	port side	bâbord
	porthole	hublot
	propeller	hélice
	prow, bow	proue
	reception desk, information desk	bureau d'information
	rescue boat	bateau de sauvetage
	rolling	roulis
to	sail [leave the harbour]	appareiller
to be	seasick	avoir le mal de mer
	seating	service de restauration
	staff captain	le commandant en second
	starboard (side)	tribord
	stern, aft	poupe
	storm warning	avis de tempête
	swell	houle
	time zone	fuseau horaire
	tonnage	tonnage
	total passenger capacity	capacité totale passagers
	weather forecast	prévisions météorologiques

7.4 Restaurant

English	**French**
The restaurant	Le restaurant
Would you like to eat?	Est-ce que tu veux manger ?

English	French
Yes, with pleasure	Oui, je veux bien
To eat	Manger
Where can we eat?	Où pouvons-nous manger ?
Where can we have lunch?	Où pouvons-nous prendre le déjeuner ?
Dinner	Le dîner
Breakfast	Le petit-déjeuner
Excuse me!	S'il vous plaît !
The menu, please	Le menu, s'il vous plaît !
Here is the menu.	Voilà le menu !
What do you prefer to eat? Meat or fish?	Qu'est-ce que tu préfères manger, de la viande ou du poisson ?
With rice	Avec du riz
With pasta	Avec des pâtes
Potatoes	Des pommes de terre
Vegetables	Des légumes
Scrambled eggs – fried eggs - or a boiled egg	Des oeufs brouillés - sur le plat - ou à la coque
Bread	Du pain
Butter	Du beurre
Salad	Une salade
Dessert	Un dessert

English	French
Fruit	Des fruits
Can I have a knife, please?	Avez-vous un couteau s'il vous plaît ?
Yes, I'll bring it to you right away.	Oui, je vous l'apporte tout de suite
A knife	Un couteau
A fork	Une fourchette
A spoon	Une cuillère
Is it a warm dish?	Est-ce que c'est un plat chaud ?
Yes, very hot also!	Oui, et très épicé également !
Warm	Chaud
Cold	Froid
Hot	Epicé
I'll have fish.	Je vais prendre du poisson !
Me too	Moi aussi

7.5 Taxi

English	French
Taxi!	Taxi !
Where would you like to go?	Où allez-vous ?
I'm going to the train station.	Je vais à la gare
I'm going to the day & night hotel.	Je vais à l'hôtel Jour et Nuit
Can you take me to the airport, please?	Pourriez-vous m'emmener à l'aéroport ?

English	French
Can you take my luggage?	Pouvez-vous prendre mes bagages ?
Is it far from here?	Est-ce que c'est loin d'ici ?
No, it's close.	Non, c'est à côté
Yes, it's a little bit further away.	Oui c'est un peu plus loin
How much will it be?	Combien cela va coûter ?
Take me there, please.	Amenez-moi ici s'il vous plaît
You go right.	C'est à droite
You go left.	C'est à gauche
It's straight on.	C'est tout droit
It's right here.	C'est ici
It's that way.	C'est par là
Stop!	Stop !
Take your time.	Prenez votre temps
Can I have a receipt, please?	Est-ce que vous pouvez me faire une note s'il vous plaît ?

7.6 Transportation

English	French
Excuse me! I'm looking for the bus stop.	S'il vous plaît ! Je cherche l'arrêt de bus
How much is a ticket to Sun City?	Quel est le prix du billet pour La ville du Soleil s'il vous plaît ?
Where does this train go, please?	Où va ce train s'il vous plaît ?

English	French
Does this train stop at Sun City?	Est-ce que ce train s'arrête dans la ville du Soleil ?
When does the train for Sun City leave?	Quand est-ce que part le train pour la ville du Soleil ?
When will this train arrive in Sun City?	Quand arrive le train pour la ville du Soleil ?
A ticket for Sun City, please	Un billet pour La ville du Soleil s'il vous plaît
Do you have the train's time table?	Avez-vous l'horaire des trains ?
Bus schedule	L'horaire des bus
Excuse me, which train goes to Sun City?	Quel est le train pour La ville du Soleil s'il vous plaît ?
This one	C'est celui-là
Thanks	Merci
Don't mention it, have a good trip!	De rien. Bon voyage !
The garage	Le garage de réparation
The petrol station	La station d'essence
A full tank, please	Le plein s'il vous plaît
Bike	Vélo
Town center	Le centre ville
Suburb	La banlieue
It is a city.	C'est une grande ville
It is a village.	C'est un village
A mountain	Une montagne

English	French
A lake	Un lac
The countryside	La campagne

7.7 Hotel

English	French
The hotel	L'hôtel
Apartment	Appartement
Welcome!	Bienvenue !
Do you have a room available?	Avez-vous une chambre libre ?
Is there a bathroom in the room?	Y a-t-il une salle de bain avec la chambre ?
Would you prefer two single beds?	Préférez-vous deux lits d'une personne ?
Do you wish to have a twin room?	Souhaitez-vous une chambre double ?
A room with bathtub – with balcony – with shower	Chambre avec bain - avec balcon - avec douche
Bed and breakfast	Chambre avec petit déjeuner
How much is it for a night?	Quel est le prix d'une nuit ?
I would like to see the room first, please	Je voudrais voir la chambre d'abord s'il vous plaît !
Yes, of course	Oui bien-sûr !
Thank you, the room is very nice.	Merci. La chambre est très bien
OK, can I reserve for tonight?	C'est bon, est-ce que je peux réserver pour ce soir ?
It's a bit too much for me, thank you.	C'est un peu trop cher pour moi, merci
Could you take care of my luggage, please?	Pouvez-vous vous occuper de mes bagages, s'il

English	French
	vous plaît ?
Where is my room, please?	Où se trouve ma chambre s'il vous plaît ?
It is on the first floor.	Elle est au premier étage
Is there a lift?	Est-ce qu'il y a un ascenseur ?
The elevator is on your left.	L'ascenseur est sur votre gauche
The elevator is on your right.	L'ascenseur est sur votre droite
Where is the laundry room, please?	Où se trouve la blanchisserie, s'il vous plaît ?
It is on the ground floor.	Elle est au rez-de-chaussée
Ground floor	Rez-de-chaussée
Bedroom	Chambre
Dry cleaner's	Pressing
Hair salon	Salon de coiffure
Car parking space	Parking pour les voitures
Let's meet in the meeting room?	On se retrouve dans la salle de réunion ?
Meeting room	La salle de réunion
The swimming pool is heated.	La piscine est chauffée
Swimming pool	La piscine
Please, wake me up at seven a.m.	Réveillez-moi à sept heures, s'il vous plaît
The key, please	La clé s'il vous plaît
The pass, please	Le pass s'il vous plaît

English	French
Are there any messages for me?	Est-ce qu'il y a des messages pour moi ?
Yes, here you are.	Oui, les voilà
No, we didn't receive anything for you.	Non, vous n'avez rien reçu
Where can I get some change?	Où puis-je faire de la monnaie ?
Please can you give me some change?	Pouvez-vous me faire de la monnaie, s'il vous plaît ?
We can make some for you. How much would you like?	Nous pouvons vous en faire. Combien voulez-vous changer ?

7.8 Camping

air bed un matelas pneumatique

an	air pump	un gonfleur
	axe [ax : US]	une hache
a	backpack (knapsack, packsack)	le sac à dos
a	billycan	une gamelle
	boots	bottes
a	camp	camp
to	camp	camper
	camp bed	lit de camp
	camper	campeur
a	campervan	un camping car
	campfire	le feu de camp
	campground	terrain de camping

	camping stove	le camping-gaz, réchaud
	campsite	terrain de camping
	campstool	siège pliant
a	caravan	une caravane
	caravan site	terrain de caravaning
	compass	boussole
	firewood	bois de chauffage
	flashlight	la lampe de poche
	flask	une gourde
a	fly sheet	le double toit, moustiquaire
	forest	bois, forêt
	grill	grill
	ground sheet	tapis de sol
	hammock	hammac
	hatchet	une hachette
	hook	crochet
	ice cooler	une glacière
	insect repellent	un insectifuge
	lamp	lampe
	lantern	lanterne
	mallet	le maillet
	matches	des allumettes
	map	une carte
a	mobile home	un mobil-home
	outdoors	en plein air

	raincoat	imperméable
	rope	corde
	sleeping bag	sac de couchage
	stake	piquet
a	tent	une tente
	pegs	les piquets
a	penknife	un canif
	pitch a tent	planter une tente
	the showers	les douches
	sleeping bag	le sac de couchage
to	take down a tent	démonter une tente
	thermos	thermos
	toilet block	les sanitaires
	torch	la lampe de poche
	trailer	caravane
	trap	piège
	water bottle	bouteille d'eau

7.9 Finance & Business

Business French

an	account	un compte
an	accountant	un comptable
an	acquisition	un rachat d'entreprise

an	advantage	un avantage
to	advertise	faire la publicité
an	advertisement	une annonce publicitaire
an	advertising campaign	une campagne publicitaire
to	afford	avoir les moyens d'acheter, pouvoir payer
the	after-sales service	le service après-vente
an	agenda	un ordre du jour
an	appointment	une nomination
to	approve	approuver, ratifier
the	Articles of Association	les statuts
an	assembly line	une chaîne de montage
to	audit the accounts	vérifier les comptes, auditer les comptes
an	auditor	un commissaire aux comptes
the	balance	le solde
a	balance sheet	un bilan
a	bank	une banque
the	assets (in a balance)	l'actif
the	liabilities	le passif
a	bankruptcy	une faillite
a	bargain	une affaire
to	be in the red (accounting)	être déficitaire
to	be in the black (accounting)	être positif
	benchmarking	un étalonnage, une référenciation
a	bill (accounting)	une note, une facture (à payer)
the	board of directors	le conseil d'administration

	bookkeeping	la comptabilité
a	book-keeper	un comptable
to	borrow	emprunter
a	branch	une agence, une succursale
a	brand	une marque
the	branding	marquage, branding
to	break a contract	violer un contrat, rompre un contrat
a	budget	un budget
the	business	le commerce, les affaires
	business is brisk	les affaires tournent
	business is slack	les affaires sont calmes
	business connections	les relations d'affaires
a	business contract	un contrat commercial
	business hours	heures ouvrable
	business intelligence	veille économique
a	business plan	un plan d'affaires
to	buy	acheter
to	buy in bulk	acheter en gros
a	buyer	un acheteur
to	cancel an order	annuler une commande
a	channel of distribution	un canal de distribution
to	charge for (payment)	faire payer
	cheap	bon marché
	co-branding	le cogriffage, alliance de marques
to	come to maturity	arriver à échéance

a	Chartered Accountant (CA)	un expert-comptable
	COD (cash on delivery)	paiement comptant à la livraison
a	commercial traveller	un représentant
a	commercial network	un réseau commercial
a	commission	une commission, une commande
to	launch a product	lancer un produit
a	company	une société
the	competition	la compétition
	competitive intelligence	veille à la concurrence
a	competitor	un concurrent
to	compete with	concourir, rivaliser avec, être en concurrence avec
to	complain	se plaindre
to	conduct a survey	mener une enquête
to	confirm	confirmer, corroborer
to	consider	considérer, examiner, songer
to	consign	expédier, envoyer
a	consignment note	un bordereau d'expédition
a	consultant	un conseiller
a	consumer	un consommateur
	consumerism	la défense du consommateur
to	convince	convaincre
a	corporation	une société
	costs	coûts
to	cost	coûter
a	creditor	un créancier

a	customer	un client
	customs duties	droits de douane
	CWO (cash with order)	paiement comptant à la commande
a	deadline	date limite
the	debt	la dette
a	debtor	débiteur
to	decide	décider
to	decrease	réduire, diminuer
to	deliver	distribuer, livrer
	delivery	distribution, livraison
the	domestic trade	le commerce intérieur
the	external trade	le commerce extérieur
the	foreign trade	le commerce extérieur
	debt collection	recouvrement de créance
a	demand	une demande
a	department	rayon, département, service
	deregulation	déréglementation
to	develop	développer
	direct mailing	publipostage direct
	direct marketing	vente directe
a	disadvantage	un inconvénient, un désavantage
a	discount	une réduction
to	dispatch	envoyer
to	distribute	distribuer
to	employ	employer

an	employee	un employé, une employée
	empowerment	renforcement d'équipe
an	equipment	un équipement, une équipage
to	establish	fonder, créer, établir
to	establish a business	créer une entreprise
to	estimate	estimer
to	exchange	échanger
the	expenses	les frais, les dépenses
	expensive	coûteux
	overhead expenses	les frais généraux
to	extend	étendre
the	facilities	équipement
	retail facilities	équipement commercial
a	feedback	un retour d'information, un feedback
to	file for bankruptcy	déposer le bilan
to	find a niche	trouver un créneau
a	firm	une entreprise, une firme
to	found a business	créer une entreprise
to	fund	financer
to	get better	s'améliorer
to	get worse	s'empirer
to	go bankrupt	faire faillite
the	goods	la marchandise, les articles
the	growth	la croissance
a	guarantee	une garantie

to	honour a contract	exécuter un contrat, réaliser un contrat
a	hoarding [GB] (= billboard)	un panneau publicitaire
a	billboard [US] (=hoarding)	un panneau publicitaire
	the head office	le siège social
to	improve	améliorer
	the income tax	l'impôt sur le revenu
to	increase	augmenter
	the industry	l'industrie
an	interest (finance)	intérêt
an	inventory	un inventaire
to	invest	investir
an	invoice	une facture (à faire payer)
to	invoice	facturer
to	join a trade union	se syndiquer
	the lay-off	le chômage temporaire
to	lend	prêter
	life cycle	cycle de vie
a	limited liability company	une société à responsabilité limitée
a	loss	une perte
to	lower	baisser
	loyalty	la fidélité
to	maintain	maintenir, entretenir
to	make money	faire de l'argent, faire des bénéfices
to	manage	gérer, diriger
	the management	la direction

the margin	la marge	
the market	le marché	
the market leader	le leader sur le marché	
a	market survey	une étude de marché
a	market share	une part de marché
to	measure	mesurer
	merchandise	les marchandises
to	merchandise	commercialiser
a	merger	une fusion d'entreprise
a	niche	un créneau
to	obtain	obtenir
an	offer	une offre
an	order	un ordre
to	order	commander, ordonner
to	organize	organiser
an	outlet	un point de vente
to	owe (I owe him 100 euros.)	devoir (Je lui dois 100 euros.)
to	own	posséder, être propriétaire
	packaging	l'emballage, le conditionnement
to	pay	payer
to	pay by installments	payer en plusieurs versements
a	payment	un paiement
	penalty	peine, condamnation
to	plan	planifier
a	preliminary contract	un avant-contrat

the price	le prix
to process	traiter, opérer, procéder
to produce	produire
a product	un produit
production	la production
profit	le bénéfice
profit margin	la marge bénéficiaire
the profitability	la rentabilité
to promote	promouvoir
a promotion	une promotion
to provide	fournir, offrir
to provide credit arrangements	offrir des facilités de crédit
a purchase	une acquisition, achat
to purchase	acheter
range	la gamme, la portée
to reach	atteindre
to recall products	retirer de produits de la vente
to recruit	recruter, enrôler
to reduce	diminuer, réduire
a reduction	une réduction, une baisse
refund	le remboursement
to refund	rembourser
the report	le rapport
reporting	le rapport, les rapports, reporting
responsibility	la responsabilité

the result	le résultat
the retailer	le détaillant
revenue	les recettes
the rise	la hausse, une augmentation
to rise	monter, augmenter, se lever
the risk	le risque, le péril
a salary	un salaire
sales	soldes
to ship	expédier
when the sales are on	au moment des soldes
a sample	un échantillon
a schedule	un horaire, un planning
to sell	vendre
a seller	un vendeur
solvent	solvable
insolvent	insolvable
in full settlement	pour solde de tout compte
a stock	un stock, une réserve
to stock up	renouveler le stock
to subsidize	subventionner
to succeed	réussir
supply	offre
the support	le soutien, un appui
a survey	une enquête
takeover	le rachat d'entreprise

	target market	le marché cible
a	trademark	une marque
	tax	impôt
	team building	renforcement d'équipe
a	think tank	une laboratoire d'idées, un groupe de réflexion
	transport	le transport
	trade	le commerce
the	trade register	le registre de commerce
a	trade show	une exposition commercial
a	trade union	un syndicat
a	trend	une tendance
the	turnover	le renouvellement, la rotation
the	turnover (accounting)	le chiffre d'affaires
un	unfair competition	une concurrence déloyale
	value for money	rapport qualité prix
to	violate a contract	violer un contrat, rompre un contrat
a	wage scale	une échelle des salaires
a	warehouse	un entrepôt
to	win	gagner
a	win-win game	un jeux gagnant-gagnant
	within 5 days	dans un délai de 5 jours

Bank and money

an (account) overdraft		découvert
account		compte
to apply for a loan		demander un prêt

to	ask for security	demander une garantie
a	ATM (automated teller machine, US), cash dispenser	un distributeur automatique
to	audit an account	vérifier un compte
a	balance	solde(d'un compe bancaire)
a	bank	banque
a	bank account	un compte bancaire
	bank card, ATM card (US)	carte bancaire
	bank cashier	caissière, caissier
	bank clerk	employé de banque
	bank manager	directeur de banque
a	bank note (GB), bill (US)	un billet de banque
	bank statement	relevé bancaire
	bank transfer	un virement bancaire
	banker	banquier
	banking	banque (organisation)
to	be in the red	être à découvert
to	borrow	emprunter
	building societies	association accès à la propriété
to	buy	acheter
to	buy on credit	acheter à crédit
	cash	du liquide
to	cash a cheque	toucher un chéquier
to	change money (into Euros)	changer de l'argent (en Euros)
	cheap	bon marché, pas cher
a	cheque (GB), check (US)	un chèque

a	coin	une pièce de monnaie
	credit	credit
	credit card	carte de crédit
	currency	devise, monnaie
a	current account (GB), checking account (US)	compte-chèques
	debit, flow	débit
to	deposit money with a bank	déposer de l'argent en banque
	debt	dette
	discount rate	taux d'escompte,, taux de remise
	exchange rate	taux de change
	expensive	cher
	financial markets	marchés financiers
	financial	financier
	foreign currency, foreign exchange	devise étrangère
	foreign exchange office, bureau de change (si)	bureau de change
to	give somebody credit	faire crédit à quelqu'un
to	go bankrupt	faire faillite
to	grant a loan	accorder un prêt
	hard currency	devise forte
	interest	intérêt
	interest rate	taux d'intérêt
to	invest	investir
to	issue a cheque	libeller un chèque
	keep the change	gardez la monnaie
a	loan	prêt, emprunt

to make out a cheque	libeller un chèque
money	monnaie, argent
mortgage	prêt immobilier, hypothèque
to open an account with	ouvrir un compte auprès de
overdrawn account	compte à découvert
to pay cash	payer en espèces
pay slip	bulletin de salaire
rate	taux
real estate loan	prêt immobilier
retail bank	banque de détail
salary	traitement
to save	économiser
saving bank	caisse d'épargne
secured credit	prêt garanti
to speculate, gamble	jouer en bourse, spéculer
to spend	dépenser
statement (of account)	relevé de compte
wages	salaire
to withdraw	retirer (l'argent)
to write a check	faire un chèque

Denominations of francs and euros:

The euro, like the *franc,* is counted in *centimes*, like our cents. Coins and bills are minted for:

1 *centime*

5 *centimes*

10 *centimes*

20 *centimes*

50 *centimes*

1 *euro*

2 *euros*

5 *euros*

10 *euros*

20 *euros*

50 *euros*

100 *euros*

200 *euros*

500 *euros*

If you can't find a price tag, just say, **"Combien coûte... ?"** as in *"Combien coûte cette robe ?"* (How much does this dress cost?) or for plural, *"Combien coûtent les bananes ?"* (How much do the bananas cost?).

If you're holding something or pointing (say you don't know the word), say: **"Combien ça coûte?"** (How much does it/this cost?).

CONCLUSION

The most challenging part of learning a foreign language is making yourself study regularly. When studying a language, repetition and regularity are vital. You could do small sessions in a week, but if you leave off until the next week, much of it will be forgotten. However, if you study a little each day and practice regularly, you'll easily remember and retain the information that you've covered. The French language is not difficult, you just have to know the basics. Once you get them, it will just be a matter of practice.

The first few times you try to speak French, you'll probably get it wrong. And that's okay!

Learning French is easy, especially if you have the opportunity to talk to native speakers They don't articulate as much, so you've got to listen carefully,but you'll get used to it with time.

The best tip I can give you is to never give up. It may sound cliché, but it is the best way to accomplish your goal..

Also, start speaking French with friends. Get them involved, because explaining your new favorite words will help consolidate your learning.

Or, if your friends aren't interested, just speak to yourself! There are so many ways to learn spoken French nowadays, such as listening to French music, watching French movies (be sure to watch the original version with English subtitles though. You need to understand it, too). An excellent way to learn is to record yourself reading or speaking French, then listen to the recordings while you walk or travel, etc. You'll improve day by day, so don't give up.

And one more thing…

Learn French at your own pace. It's easier to learn a language with passion!

Part 2: French Short Stories

8 Simple and Captivating Stories for Effective French Learning for Beginners

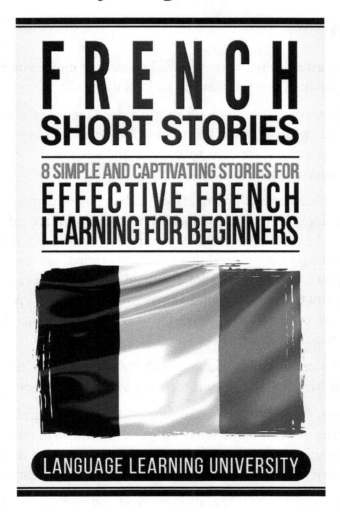

Introduction

Have you ever tried to learn a foreign language while watching movies or cartoons? And have you stopped because it was too hard you felt that you had not evolved?

Do not get discouraged, because learning with short stories is more efficient and easier due to the fact you can dive into the universe of the history itself and you will not go overboard as you will progress at your own pace. You are free to re-read and review the chapters to form a better understanding of the language if you want to.

Learning through short stories is much more effective than any other modality. The most sensible recommendation would surely be to read as much as possible! Similarly, if you want to continue to learn more vocabulary and improve your ability to express yourself in a foreign language, whether written or spoken, we strongly recommend that you read original stories or novels. You will dive into the characters but you will also learn a lot about how to talk and even use certain expressions. The activity that allows you to improve continuously in written or oral French is reading. Practiced during our school course or even after, it is the activity that brings back the most notions: linguistic, grammar, conjugation and spelling.

The advantage of short stories is that you can both follow the story and remember each event without having the impression that the story is too long or the story is boring.

This book contains 8 short stories with both the original version and the English translation on the same page. This is an effective technique for learning new words and phrases as both versions are available at a glance. In this way if we do not understand a passage that we have just read the translation is right next to it, which avoids having to search for their meaning!

The texts are not complicated and any beginner can read and understand the stories. They are not too long because it is better to have small, captivating stories than to dive into a long novel if you are there to learn French.

If you want to concentrate and to escape completely, it is recommended to find a calm environment, without any external presence to maximize your ability to make the most of what you are reading.

How to read effectively

If you chose this book because you want to learn French by reading short stories, then here are some tips for a better reading experience:

Read the whole story

When you first read a story in a language you do not understand, and you do not understand what you are reading, it does not matter. Nothing is alarming about that, it's normal. The mistake not to do is to give up and turn back to the beginning.

Indeed, read the story once or twice. The purpose of short stories is to give you the ability to reread and review what you did not understand without having to go back too far in history.

As you read you will realize that you are comprehending much faster and much more than at first reading. But there is another method.

Take small breaks

You do not have to force yourself to read all the stories at once or to finish one when you do not understand it. Do not hesitate to stop from time to time (but not too much, it will break your concentration) and see or search for the meaning of words or phrases you do not understand. This will help you move faster than if you read the whole story without really understanding the background. Do not hesitate to take a tour in the Vocabulaire/Vocabulary section if there are words that escape you.

Chapter 1 – Une nouvelle vie

« Debout, Mathieu ! dit une voix sourde.

– Quelle heure est-il ? demandai-je à ma mère qui me réveillait.

– Il est huit heures, je te réveille comme tu me l'as demandé hier soir. Dépêche-toi de t'habiller.

– D'accord. »

Je m'appelle Mathieu, j'ai dix-neuf ans et je viens d'obtenir une bourse pour continuer mes études à l'étranger. Je suis assez grand, je mesure un mètre quatre-vingts, les cheveux un peu ondulés, noirs et les yeux noisette. J'ai quelques taches de rousseurs sur le visage, ce qui me donne un air sauvage comme le dit ma grande sœur, Marie, qui elle aussi est partie étudier à l'étranger il y a deux ans.

« Mathieu, dépêche-toi !

– Ok, m'man, j'arrive dans cinq minutes ! »

Ma mère s'appelle Zoé et mon père Henri. Ils sont mariés depuis vingt-cinq ans et ont trois enfants dont ma grande sœur Marie, mon petit frère Quentin et moi.

Mon avion décolle ce soir à vingt heures. Maman est stressée, comme d'habitude. D'autant plus que j'ai encore des achats à faire avant de fermer définitivement mes bagages. J'ai déjà rangé toutes mes affaires personnelles hier soir mais, avec maman, on n'est jamais sûr de rien. Elle pense toujours à tout et je ne vais pas m'en plaindre.

Quand je descends dans la cuisine, papa finit encore son café et Quentin joue avec son lait et quelques biscottes tartinées de Nutella.

« Bonjour !

– Bonjour fiston !

– Assieds-toi, il reste du fromage dans le frigo si tu ne veux pas manger sucré.

– C'est impressionnant de voir que tu lis dans les pensées maman, merci !

– Je suis ta mère, c'est normal, je te connais comme ma poche*. »

Papa se lève et me tapote gentillement la tête. C'est le genre de geste affectif qu'il ne se permet jamais. Il doit être un peu triste de mon départ, mais il a trop de fierté pour me le dire en face. D'autant plus qu'il est timide et réservé, ce geste est déjà un gros effort de sa part.

Je termine vite fait mon petit déjeuner. Je n'ai pas très faim ce matin, c'est sûrement l'excitation du voyage qui me coupe l'appétit.

Je me prépare pour aller faire quelques emplettes histoire de ne rien oublier. Je vérifie ce qu'il manque dans mes affaires. Je devrais sûrement acheter une nouvelle brosse à dents, ça ne sert à rien d'emmener la vieille brosse que j'ai ci.

Il est presque quatorze heures quand je finis de préparer mes bagages. Sans oublier toutes les choses que tante Marguerite m'a demandé d'acheter pour elle, il y en a toute une longue liste.

Je m'allonge un moment sur le lit et j'attends.

Je vais bientôt partir. Je suis à la fois triste et excité. Triste parce que mes parents et mes frères et sœurs vont me manquer. Et excité parce que je vais bientôt découvrir de nouveaux horizons, vivre de nouvelles choses.

Je rêvasse encore un instant avant que papa ne m'appelle du hall pour me dire qu'on part bientôt. J'arrange mes cheveux ébouriffés et je descends les escaliers en trombe avec mon bagage à main.

Tout le monde est habillé. C'est un samedi, Quentin n'a donc pas d'école.

Papa démarre la voiture, maman à côté de lui et nous deux derrière, comme d'habitude.

Il n'y a pas eu trop d'embouteillages, il faisait chaud et je regrette un peu d'avoir porté un manteau. Il est presque seize heures lorsqu'on arrive à l'aéroport.

Maman sort mon passeport et le met dans ma poche pour ne pas que je le perde.

Je dois me présenter à l'embarquement et papa m'y accompagne.

Tout est là. Ils impriment mon billet d'avion et je fais un peu la queue en attendant mon tour.

Je rejoins papa le temps qu'ils finissent la paperasse et lui demande où sont maman et Quentin. Il me dit qu'elle est allée acheter à boire et à manger au cas où j'aurais un petit creux car l'avion aura du retard. Justement les voilà qui arrivent.

« Tiens, je t'ai acheté des chips si tu as envie de grignoter.

– Merci maman !

– Alors ? Prêt ?

– Bien sûr ! Ne fais pas cette tête, avec la technologie d'aujourd'hui, on pourra se parler tous les jours.

– Je sais, je ne m'en fais pas trop. »

On annonce le départ et les passagers se hâtent à l'embarquement.

Mon cœur est lourd, je serre mes proches un par un. Quentin a les yeux larmoyants, papa aussi même s'il essaye de le cacher en essuyant de temps en temps ses yeux.

Maman me fait un bisou sur chaque joue et me dit bon voyage avant d'essuyer une larme.

Je n'ai pas de voix, je me contente de sourire.

Encore une fois, je suis à la fois triste heurex. C'est toujours un peu triste de quitter les gens que l'on aime, même si c'est temporaire.

Je me dirige vers la salle d'embarquement et me retourne pour leur faire signe de la main en souriant.

Une fois dans l'avion, je prends une profonde inspiration.

Il doit être vingt heures quand l'avion décolle enfin.

C'est le début d'une nouvelle vie !

"Wake up Mathieu," said a dull voice.

" What time is it?" I asked my mother.

"It is 8 o'clock. You asked me to wake you up yesterday night. Hurry up and get dressed.

' Okay. Thank you.'

My name is Mathieu, I'm 19 years old and I just got a scholarship to continue my studies abroad. I am really tall, 1.80m tall, black hair, a little wavy, with hazel eyes. I have some freckles on my face, which gives me a wild look as my sister Marie used to tell me. She also went to study abroad 2 years ago.

"Mathieu, hurry up!"

'Ok, mom, I'm coming in five minutes!'

My mother's name is Zoé and my father is Henri. They have been married for 25 years and have three children, including my older sister Marie, my little brother Quentin and me.

My plane takes off tonight at 8 pm so Mom is stressed as usual, especially since I still have purchases to make before closing my bags for good. I have already packed all my personal belongings last night but with Mom we can never be sure of anything. She always thinks about everything and I will never complain.

When I go down to the kitchen, Dad is finishing his coffee and Quentin is playing with his milk and a few crackers that he has spread with Nutella.

'Hello!'

'Hello, son!'

'Sit down, there is cheese in the fridge if you do not want to eat sweet.'

'It's awesome to see you've got some mind-reading powers, Mom. Thanks!'

'I am your mother; it's obvious, I know you like the back of my hand, Mathieu.'

Dad gets up and pats my head. That's the kind of affectional gesture he never lets himself do. He must be a little sad about my departure but he has too much pride to say it to my face. Especially since he is shy and reserved, his gesture earlier was already a big effort on his part.

I finish my breakfast quickly. I'm not very hungry this morning; it's probably the excitement of the trip that cuts my appetite.

I'm getting ready to go shopping to be sure not to forget anything. I check what's missing in my stuff, I should probably buy a new toothbrush. I'm not going to lug around my old toothbrush.

It is almost 2 pm when I finished preparing my own luggage, not to mention all the things Aunt Marguerite asked me to buy, which is a whole long list.

I dozed off for a moment on the bed and I waited.

I'll be leaving soon. I feel both sad and excited. Sad because my parents and siblings will miss me. And happy because I'm going to see new horizons, discover new things.

Dad woke me up from my daydreams and told me we were leaving soon. I arranged my ruffled hair and ran down the stairs with my carry-on luggage.

Everyone is dressed, and it was a Saturday, so my little brother did not have school. Dad starts the car; Mom sits next to him and us behind as usual. There's not much traffic, it's hot and I regret a little wearing this coat. It is almost 4 pm when we arrive at the airport.

Mom takes out my passport and puts it in my pocket so I do not lose it. I have to go to boarding and Dad accompanies me. Everything is there; they print my plane ticket and I follow a little queue waiting for my turn.

I join Daddy when they finish the paperwork and ask him where Mom and Quentin are. He tells me that she went to get something to drink and eat in case I need a snack because the plane will be late. "Here they come.'

'Here, I bought you chips if you want to nibble.'

'Thanks Mom!'

'So? Ready?'

'Of course! Do not do that face, with today's technology, we can talk every day.'

'I know, I am not worried about you.'

They announce the departure and the passengers hastily embark. My heart is heavy. I squeeze my loved ones one by one. My little brother has tearful eyes, Daddy too, even if he tries to hide it by wiping his eyes which are already red.

Mom gives me a kiss and tells me to have a good trip before wiping a tear from her right cheek. I do not have any words, so I just smile.

To be honest, I'm happy, happy but also sad because it's always a bit sad to leave the people we love.

I head to the departure lounge and turn around to wave at them, smiling.

Once on the plane, I doze off and take a deep breath. It's the beginning of a new life!

Vocabulaire / Vocabulary

lycée - high school

bourse - scholarship

étranger - foreign

frères et sœurs - brothers and sisters / siblings

mère - mother

grand - tall

cheveux - hair

ondulé(s) - wavy

noir(s) - black

visage - face

taches de rousseur - freckles

air - look

sauvage - wild

café - coffee

biscottes - rusks

petit déjeuner - breakfast

fiston - son (informal)

affectif – affectionate, loving

geste - gesture

« *Je te connais comme ma poche* »* - literally "I know you as my pocket" is used in French to say you know someone like you created them – "I know you as the back of my hand"

Questions

1 - Quel âge a Mathieu?

a. 16

b. 20

c. 30

d. 19

2 - Quel est le prénom du père de Mathieu ?

a. Henri

b. Samuel

c. Antoine

d. Stéphane

3 - Comment s'appelle la mère de Mathieu ?

a. Solange

b. Adèle

c. Zoé

d. Anastasia

4 - Combien de frères et de sœurs Mathieu a-t-il ?

a. Deux frères

b. Deux sœurs

c. Deux frères et une sœur

d. Une sœur et un frère

5 - A quelle heure part l'avion de Mathieu ?

a. A 18h

b. A 14h

c. A 8h du matin

d. A 09h00

6 - Comment s'appelle le petit frère de Mathieu ?

7 - Pourquoi le petit frère de Mathieu n'a-t-il pas d'école ce jour-là ?

8 - Qu'est-ce que la mère de Mathieu lui a acheté à l'aéroport ?

9 - Comment Mathieu se sent-il ?

10 - A quelle heure l'avion décolle-t-il ?

1 - How old is Mathieu?

a. 16

b. 20

c. 30

d. 19

2 - What's the name of Mathieu's father?

a. Henri

b. Samuel

c. Antoine

d. Stéphane

3 - What's Mathieu's mom's name?

a. Solange

b. Adèle

c. Zoé

d. Anastasia

4 - How many brothers and sisters Mathieu has?

a. Two brothers

b. Two sisters

c. Two brothers and one sister

d. One sister and one brother

5 - What time does Mathieu's plane leave?

a. A 20pm

b. At 2pm

c. At 8 o'clock in the morning

d. At 09:00 am

6 - What is the name of Mathieu's little brother?

7 - Why Mathieu's little brother does not have school that day?

8 - What did Mathieu's mother buy him at the airport?

9 - How does Mathieu feel?

10 - What time does the plane take off?

Réponses

1 - d

2 - a

3 - c

4 - d

5 - a

6 - Le petit frère de Mathieu s'appelle Quentin.

7 - Le petit frère de Mathieu n'a pas école ce jour-là parce que c'est un samedi.

8 - La mère de Mathieu lui a acheté des chips à l'aéroport.

9 - Mathieu est à la fois excité et triste.

10 - L'avion décolle à 20h.

Answers

1 - d

2 - a

3 - c

4 - d

5 - a

6 - Mathieu's little brother is named Quentin.

7 - Mathieu's little brother does not have to go to school that day because it's Saturday.

8 - Mathieu's mother bought him crisps at the airport.

9 - Mathieu is excited and sad at the same time.

10 - The plane takes off at 8pm.

Chapter 2 – Un petit tour

Cela va faire trois jours que je suis descendu de l'avion qui m'a emmené loin de chez moi et les cours ont commencé aujourd'hui. Je suis impatient de rencontrer tous mes nouveaux professeurs. J'ai choisi la communication parce que j'aime tout simplement ça et je trouve plus facile et agréable d'apprendre quelque chose que l'on aime.

Je loge dans une chambre à l'est du campus et mon camarade de chambre s'appelle Zack. Il vient de Marseille. On s'est très bien entendu dés notre première rencontre.

Zack est assez costaud , c'est un sportif. Il a les cheveux blonds, des yeux verts et porte souvent des joggings ou des shorts.

La journée de cours est terminée alors on en profite un peu pour flemmarder dans notre chambre.

Je lis un livre d'Edgar Allan Poe tandis que lui joue avec son ballon sur son lit. Il l'envoie en l'air et le rattrape. Il n'est pas très bavard aujourd'hui et ça m'arrange car quand il s'y met, c'est une véritable radio. Pour le moment, j'ai juste envie de lire et de me reposer.

« C'était une longue journée, non ? me dit-il.

– Mhhh, pas vraiment, je n'ai pas eu l'impression de m'ennuyer pendant les cours.

– Haha, c'est toujours comme ça au début. Après, c'est la routine qui prend le dessus. Mais c'est bien d'être motivé. »

Je me lève et cherche de l'argent dans les poches de mon jeans sale. Zack arrête de lancer le ballon en l'air et me regarde.

« Tu vas quelque part ?

– Oui, j'ai quelques courses à faire. J'ai la dalle.

– Tu peux m'acheter un paquet de chewing-gum s'il-te-plaît ? A la menthe. Je te paierai quand tu reviendras.

– OK, autre chose ?

– Mhhh, non ce sera tout. Merci »

J'enfile un sweat bleu. Il fait frais dehors et je n'ai pas envie de tomber malade en plein début des cours. D'autant plus que je ne suis pas encore habitué au décalage horaire et que je suis encore un peu fatigué de mon voyage.

Mon emploi du temps est assez libre. Je ne suis pas submergée de cours tous les jours, ce qui me donne l'occasion de faire autre chose en parallèle. Pourquoi pas un petit job ? Ce serait intéressant, mais je dois encore m'adapter au rythme de vie étudiant. Peut-être que d'ici un mois ou deux, j'envisagerai de travailler à côté.

Je marche le long des trottoirs et cherche une supérette dans les parages. J'ai dû marcher une bonne quinzaine de minutes avant d'en trouver une.

Je m'achète des chips, une cannette de Pepsi et des cigarettes, sans oublier le paquet de chewing-gum que Zack m'a demandé de rapporter.

Je parcours les rayons afin de trouver quelques sucreries pour mes révisions du soir.

Je passe à la caisse, le monsieur me dit bonjour et prend les sous que je lui tends.

« Ce sera tout ?

– Oui.

– Merci, monsieur. Bonne journée.

– Bonne journée ! »

En sortant, je me rends compte que c'était très peu de courses pour quand même quinze minutes de marche. Je devrais peut-être acheter autre chose ? Non. De toute façon ce n'est pas grave, je peux revenir de temps en temps, ça me fera un peu de sport.

J'ouvre ma canette de Pepsi et prend une gorgée tout en continuant de marcher jusqu'à ma chambre.

Quand j'entre, la porte n'est pas fermée. C'est sûrement moi qui l'ai oublié en sortant vu que Zack dort comme un bébé sur son lit. Quelle marmotte* celui-là.

Je dépose mes courses sur la table et je sors mes cahiers pour revoir mes cours d'aujourd'hui. Zack a raison, ce n'est pas quelque chose que je fais en plein semestre généralement. C'est sûrement la motivation des premiers jours et de ce nouveau cadre. Qu'importe, j'ouvre mes cahiers et je plonge dans mes bouquins. De toute façon, je n'ai personne à qui parler vu que Zack dort. Ça me fait un peu de calme pour réviser.

It's been three days since I got off the plane that took me away from home and the classes starts today. I'm looking forward to meeting all my new teachers. I chose communication because I like it and I find it's easier to learn something we like.

I'm staying in a room on the east side of the campus and my roommate's name is Zack ; he's from Marseille and we've gotten along very well since we met.

Zack is quite sturdy since he plays sports, he has blond hair, green eyes and often wears joggings or shorts.

The classes are over so we enjoy loafing in our room.

I read a book by Edgar Allan Poe while he plays with his ball on his bed. He sends it in the air and returns it once in his hands. He is not very talkative today and it is ok for me because when he starts, he is a real radio and for the moment I just want to read and rest.

'It was a long day, right?' he asked me.

'Mhhh, not really, I did not feel bored during class.'

'Haha, it's always like that at the beginning, after, the routine takes over. But it's good to be motivated.'

I get up and look for money in the pockets of my dirty jeans. Zack stops throwing the ball in the air and looks at me.

'You're going somewhere?'

'Yes, I have some shopping to do. I'm starving.'

'Can you buy me a pack of chewing gum please? Mint-flavoured. I'll pay you when you come back.'

'Ok, something else?'

'Mhhh, no that's all.'

I put on a blue sweatshirt; it's cool outside, I do not want to get sick in the beginning of classes, especially since I still have jet lag and I'm still a little tired from my trip.

My schedule is pretty free, I'm not overwhelmed with classes every day, which gives me the opportunity to do something else in parallel. Why not a small job? It would be interesting but I still have to adapt to the rhythm of student life. Maybe in a month or two I'll consider working a little bit.

I walk along the sidewalks and look for a supermarket nearby. I have to walk a good fifteen minutes before finding one.

I buy chips, a can of Pepsi and cigarettes. Not to mention the pack of chewing gum that Zack asked me to bring back.

I scroll the shelves to find some sweets as provisions for the evening.

I go to the cash register; the gentleman welcomes me by saying hello and takes the notes that I hand him over.

'That will be all?'

'Yes.'

'Thank you sir. Have a good day.'

'Have a good day !'

While leaving, I realized that it was more than fifteen minutes of walking. Maybe I should buy something else? Anyway, it did not matter, I could come back from time to time, it will be some exercise.

I open my Pepsi can and take a sip while continuing to walk to my room.

When I enter, the door is not closed; it is probably me who forgot to close it when going out as Zack sleeps like a baby on his bed. What a log that one.

I put my groceries on the table and I take my notebooks to see today's classes. Zack is right; it's not something I usually do in the middle of the semester, it's probably the motivation of the early days and the new landscape. No matter, I open my notebooks and dive into my books. Anyway, I have no one to talk to because Zack is still sleeping; it gives me a bit of calm to revise.

Résumé

Cela va faire trois jours que Mathieu est arrivé à destination et maintenant il commence les cours. Il a un camarade de chambre. Il s'appelle Zack et il vient de Marseille. Mathieu s'entend bien avec Zack. Pour passer le temps, Mathieu décide de sortir faire quelques achats et en profiter pour se familiariser avec son nouvel environnement. Une fois de retour, il profite du calme et de sa motivation pour réviser un peu.

Summary

It's been three days since Mathieu arrived at his destination and now he's starting classes. He has a roommate. His name is Zack and he comes from Marseille. Mathieu gets on well with Zack. To pass time, Mathieu decides to go out to do some shopping and take the opportunity to get acquainted with his new environment. Once back, he enjoys the calm and some motivation to study a little.

Vocabulaire / Vocabulary

trois jours - three days

chez moi - home

cours - classes

professeurs - teachers

apprendre - to learn

quelque chose - something

chambre - room

campus - campus

camarade de chambre - Roommate

rencontre - meeting (from the verb « *rencontrer* » or to meet)

flemmarder - to loaf

ballon - ball

pas très bavard - not very talkative

j'ai la dalle - I'm hungry (informal)

menthe - mint

décalage horaire - jet lag

voyage - trip

emploi du temps - schedule

trottoirs - sidewalks

supérette - minimarket

canette - can

quelle marmotte* - literally "what a marmot". It is used to call someone who sleeps most of the time, just as a marmot – Sleeping like a log, like a baby

semestre - semester

Questions

1 - L'histoire se passe combien de temps après l'arrivée de Mathieu en France ?

a. Une semaine

b. Deux semaines

c. Trois jours

d. Un mois

2 - Quelle filière Mathieur a-t-il choisie ?

a. Le droit

b. La communication

c. La médecine

d. La gestion

3 - Comment s'appelle le colocataire de Mathieu ?

a. Zack

b. Jerry

c. Carter

d. John

4 - D'où vient Zack ?

a. Zack vient de Montréal.

b. Zack vient de Marseille.

c. Zack vient de Paris.

d. Zack vient du Mexique.

5 - Quel sport Zack pratique-t-il ?

a. Zack joue au football.

b. Zack joue au tennis.

c. Zack joue au basketball.

d. Zack joue au handball.

6 - Où va Mathieu ?

a. Il va au terrain de basketball.

b. Il va à la piscine.

c. Il va en cours.

d. Il va faire quelques courses.

7 - Que lui demande d'acheter Zack ?

8 - De quel couleur est le sweat de Mathieu ?

9 - Combien de temps Mathieu marche-t-il avant de trouver une supérette ?

10 - Qu'est-ce que Mathieu achète dans la supérette ?

11 - Que fais Mathieu une fois dans sa chambre ?

Questions

1- How long after Mathieu's arrival in France does the story takes place?

a-One week

b-Two weeks

c-Three days

d-One month

2-What did Mathieu choose?

a- Law

b-Communication

c-Medicine

d-Management

3-What's the name of Mathieu's roommate?

a- Zack

b-Jerry

c-Carter

of John

4-Where does Zack come from?

a-Zack comes from Montreal

b-Zack comes from Marseille

c-Zack comes from Paris

d-Zack comes from Mexico

5-What sport does Zack do?

a-Zack is playing football

b-Zack plays tennis

c-Zack plays basketball

d-Zack plays handball

6-What does Zack ask him to buy?

7-What color is Mathieu's sweatshirt?

8-How long does Mathieu walk before he finds a supermarket?

9-What does Mathieu buy in the supermarket?

10-What does Mathieu do once in his room?

Réponses

1 - c

2 - b

3 - a

4 - b

5 - c

6 - Zack lui demande d'acheter un paquet de chewing-gum à la menthe.

7 - Le sweat de Mathieu est de couleur bleue.

8 - Mathieu marche une quinzaine de minutes avant de trouver une supérette.

9 - Mathieu achète des chips, une canette de Pepsi, cigarettes et les chewing-gums de Zack.

10 - Une fois dans sa chambre, Mathieu révise.

Answers

1 C

2-b

3-a

4-b

5-c

6-Zack asks him to buy a packet of mint chewing gum.

7-Mathieu's sweatshirt is blue.

8-Mathieu walks for about fifteen minutes before finding a small supermarket.

9- Mathieu buys chips, a can of Pepsi, cigarettes and chewing gum from Zack.

10-Once in his room, Mathieu revises.

Chapter 3 – Vieilles habitudes

C'était un après-midi comme les autres. Nous n'avions pas cours ce jour-là et j'en ai profité pour me reposer. Zack et moi habitions dans une chambre d'étudiant banale, avec des lits parallèles et des étagères pour ranger nos affaires personnelles. Zack dormait en face de moi. Il laissait défiler les actualités Facebook sur l'écran de son téléphone tandis que j'essayais de dormir, en vain.

« C'est fou ce que je me trouve maigre. J'ai perdu pas mal de poids depuis mon arrivée ici.

– Tu travailles trop, ménage-toi de temps en temps, marmonna-t-il.

– Il faut bien se faire un peu d'argent de poche, tout le monde n'a pas la chance d'avoir des parents comme les tiens.

– C'est pas faux, mais si tu te trouves maigre, fait un peu de sport. C'est toujours mieux que de rester enfermé ici.

– Tu fais quoi comme activité physique à part le basket ?

– Ma session d'entraînement habituelle est de quatre-vingt minutes. J'ai une routine de vingt minutes sur le tapis de course, une heure pour les poids libres et dix minutes d'abdos que je fais tous les jours. C'est parfois dur de s'y tenir parce que je suis crevé après les cours, donc je n'en fais plus tous les jours. Les weekends où les jours où je ne fais rien de spécial, je vais au terrain m'échauffer un peu, ça me déstresse aussi quoi. Pourquoi ?

– Non, juste comme ça. Je ne suis pas trop musculation. Je voudrais juste une activité physique régulière. J'ai à peine 20 ans et je me sens déjà vieux. »

J'ébouriffe mes cheveux. J'ai envie de faire autre chose que de travailler comme serveur au fast-food et aller en cours. Je n'ai pas de vie sociale du tout, Zack dirait que je suis un « *no-life* » , mais au fond, ça ne me gêne pas plus que ça. Je n'ai pas besoin d'une tonne d'amis sans valeur.

« J'ai fait du basketball au collège.

– Ah oui ? Eh bien, tu parles d'une nouvelle ! Pourquoi t'as arrêté ?

– Je ne sais plus trop, je faisais des matchs pendant les heures de pause, et j'étais plutôt… très enthousiaste et je prenais ça trop à cœur. Je ne supportais pas de perdre, alors que tu sais, dans ce genre d'activité tu ne peux pas toujours gagner.

– Mais il faut le prendre comme un loisir et non une compétition. Sinon, c'est sûr, tu te lasseras aussi vite que tu as commencé.

– C'est peut-être ça… »

Zack se lève, enfile un maillot « Jordan » et ramasse son ballon.

« Moi, je vais me faire un petit match amical. Je vais au terrain de basketball du campus voir s'il y a des joueurs.

– Maintenant ?

– Ouais, pourquoi ? Tu veux venir ?

– Je ne sais pas, ça fait longtemps.

– Fais pas ta poule mouillée, le basketball ça ne se perd pas, allez !

– Mais je n'ai pas de tenue appropriée.

– Je te filerai un de mes maillots, ils sont un peu larges pour toi mais bon…

Il cherche un maillot dans son placard et me tend un autre numéro vingt-trois de couleur rouge.

– Je pense que je ne vais pas porter de short mais juste un jean. Je vais juste jouer un peu, je ne pense pas tenir pendant un match entier.

– Comme tu veux, allez, on y va !

Il faisait assez chaud dehors, il était quatorze heures trente, il n'y avait pas beaucoup d'étudiants dans la cour. Pendant qu'on marchait, j'entendais déjà des bruits de rebonds de ballon au fur et à mesure que l'on se rapprochait du terrain. Il y avait d'autres étudiants qui jouaient. Je me sentais nerveux, et si j'étais nul ? Ce serait gênant, surtout s'il y avait du monde. J'ai commencé à hésiter. Mais en repensant à ce que Zack avait dit, il fallait se lâcher un peu, se relaxer et s'amuser. Demain, j'irai de nouveau à mes cours de communication, et après je passerai au travail pour finir tard et rentrer au campus lire un livre avant de m'endormir.

« Salut les gars, on peut se joindre à vous ? demande Zack en tapant dans la main d'un mec barbu.

– Ouais, Maxime et Franck allaient justement partir.

– Cool ! »

Je me souviens des règles de base mais je ne sais pas si je sais encore bien jouer.

Zack commence avec le ballon en main. Nous somme quatre dont Zack et moi contre Akim et Michaël. Zack dribble un moment avant de me passer le ballon, je dribble maladroitement mais rien de honteux.

Je lui file le ballon et il lance un trois points qu'il réussit.

« Pas mal pour un basketteur rouillé. », me lance-t-il.

Après à peine quinze minutes de jeu, je suis vraiment essoufflé. Ils jouent bien trop vite pour moi. Je suis quand même le rythme, et le score est assez serré, même si c'est Zack qui a marqué la majorité de nos paniers.

Après trente minutes, je sors.

Je me suis vraiment amusé, mais mes poumons crient au secours. Je n'ai pas autant transpiré depuis le collège.

« Je suis lessivé, je vais rentrer. C'était sympa.

– OK. Enrique c'est ton tour ! » dit Zack tout en lançant le ballon à Akim.

Je rentre au campus en marchant lentement, reprenant mon souffle. Demain j'aurai sûrement des courbatures, mais ça en valait la peine : je me sens déjà plus vif, en bonne santé, même si c'est sûrement que dans ma tête.

Je souris à cette idée. Pour moi, c'est le genre de journée animée et de vieilles habitudes que je n'ai pas à regretter.

It was an ordinary afternoon. We had no class that day and I took the opportunity to rest. Zack and I lived in a basic student room, with parallel beds and shelves to store our belongings. Zack was sleeping in front of me. He was reading news on his Facebook timeline on his phone screen while I was trying to sleep, to no avail.

'It's crazy how I find myself skinny. I lost a lot of weight since I arrived here.'

'You work too much, take care of yourself from time to time,' he mumbled.

'Got to get a little pocket money, not everyone has the chance to have parents like yours.'

'It's not wrong, but if you find yourself thin, do some sports. It's always better than staying locked here.'

'What do you do as a physical activity other than basketball?'

'My usual training session is eighty minutes. I have a twenty-minute routine on the treadmill, an hour for free weights and ten minutes of abs that I do every day. It's a little confusing when I'm tired after classes so I do not do it anymore. And the weekends or some days when I do nothing special I go to the basketball court, get a bit warmed up, it helps me unwind. Why?'

'No, just like that. I am not so muscular. I would like a regular physical activity, I'm barely 20 years old and I feel old.'

I ruffle my hair, I want to do something other than working as a waiter at the fast food stand and going to class. I do not have a social life at all, Zack would call me a "Nolife," but basically it does not bother me more than that. I do not need a ton of worthless friends.

'I did basketball in middle school.'

'Ah yes? Well, that's news! Why did you stop?'

'I don't really know, I played games during breaks, and I was rather ... very enthusiastic and I took it too much to heart. I can not stand to lose while, you know, in this kind of activity you can not always win.'

'But it must be taken as a hobby and not a competition. Otherwise, for sure, you'll get tired as fast as you started.'

'It may be that ...'

Zack gets up, puts on a jersey and picks up his ball.

'I'd like to go for a little friendly match. I will go to the campus basketball court to see if there are players.'

'Now?'

'Yeah, why? You want to come?'

'I do not know, it's been a long time.'

'Don''t be such a wimp, you can't forget how to play basketball, come on!'

'But I do not have proper attire.'

'I will loan you one of my jerseys ; they are a bit wide for you but hey ...'

He looks for a jersey in his shelf and hands me another red number 23.

'I think I will not wear shorts, just jeans. I'm just going to play a bit, I do not think I'm going to play for the whole match.'

'You do as you like, come on!'

It was quite hot outside, it was 14:30 in the afternoon, so there were not many students in the yard. As we walked, I heard the sound of bouncing basketballs as we got closer to the field. There were other students playing. I felt nervous, and what if I was lame? It would be embarrassing especially if there were people. I started hesitating. But thinking back to what Zack told me, I had to let go a little, relax and have fun. Tomorrow I would go back to my communication classes and then I'd go to work, finish late and return to the campus to read a book before falling asleep.

'Hey guys, can we join you?' Zack asks, giving a high five to a bearded guy.

'Yeah, Maxime and Franck were just leaving.'

'Cool !'

'I remember the basics and the rules but I do not know if I'm still good at practice.'

Zack starts with the ball in hand. We are four including Zack and me against Akim and Michaël. Zack dribbles for a moment before passing me the ball ; I dribbled awkwardly but nothing shameful.

I give him back the ball and he throws a three-point, succeeding.

'Not bad for a rusty basketball player. » he says,

After just fifteen minutes of match I'm out of breath, but really. They play too fast for me, I'm keeping the pace and the score is quite tight, even if it is Zack who scored the majority of our points.

After thirty minutes I leave the court.

I really enjoyed it but my lungs scream for help. I have not been so sweaty since middle school.

'I'm wiped, I'll go home. It was nice.'

'OK. Enrique, it's your turn!' said Zack while throwing the ball at Akim.

I go back to campus walking slowly, catching my breath. Tomorrow I will probably feel stiff but it was worth it. I already feel more alive, more healthy even if it's probably just in my head.

I smile at this idea. For me it's the kind of hectic day and old habits that I do not have to regret.

Résumé

C'était un de ces après-midi où Mathieu reste dans sa chambre à lire ou à dormir avec Zack juste en face de lui. Mais ce jour là, il se sent nostalgique alors il commence à parler de sport à Zack. Zack, lui, est fanatique de basket, du coup il lui propose de venir jouer avec lui. Mathieu hésite un peu mais il n'a pas grand-chose d'intéressant à faire et faire un peu de sport ne lui ferait pas de mal. Ils jouent une demi-partie avant que Mathieu ne sorte. Ses poumons lui ont rappelé ses années d'inactivité sportive. Cependant, il s'est amusé, alors il compte reprendre le basketball de temps en temps.

Summary

It was one of those afternoons when Mathieu stayed in his room reading or sleeping with Zack right in front of him. But that day, he feels nostalgic so he starts talking about sports to Zack. Zack is a basketball fanatic so he invites him to play with him. Mathieu hesitates a bit but he does not have much interest in doing anything else and a little sport does not hurt. They play half a game before Mathieu leaves. His lungs reminded him of his years of physical inactivity. However, he had fun so he plans to play basketball from time to time.

Vocabulaire / Vocabulary

après-midi - afternoon

lit(s) - bed(s)

parallèle(s) - parallel

affaires personnelles - personal belongings

actualités - news

en vain - in vain

maigre - thin

entraînement - training

Questions

1 - Que fais Mathieu cet après-midi-là ?

a. Il essaye de dormir.

b. Il lit un livre.

c. Il joue avec son téléphone.

---

d. Il regarde un film sur son ordinateur.

2 - Que fais Zack à côté ?

a. Zack joue avec son ballon de basket.

b. Zack dort.

c - Zack joue avec son téléphone.

d - Zack est sorti.

3 - Quand est-ce que Zack joue au basketball ?

a. Après les cours

b. Avant les cours

c. Quand il n'a pas cours

d. Pendant le weekend

4 - De quelle couleur est le maillot que Zack donne à Mathieu ?

a. Rouge

b. Bleu

c. Jaune

d. Orange

5 - Quel indice indique à Mathieu que des gens jouent au terrain ?

a. Il entend des gens parler.

b. Il entend des gens rire.

c. Il entend les rebonds du ballon.

d. Il entend des bruits de pas.

6 - Comment s'appellent les adversaires de Zack et Mathieu ?

7 - Pourquoi Mathieu et Zack peuvent-ils prendre le relais de la partie ?

8 - Pourquoi Mathieu arrête-t-il de jouer ?

9 - Comment se sent Mathieu après le match ?

10 - Est-ce que Mathieu compte reprendre le basketball ? Pourquoi ?

Questions

1-What is Mathieu doing this afternoon?

a-He tries to sleep

b-He reads a book

c-He plays with his phone

d-He's watching a movie on his computer

2-What is Zack doing next to him?

a-Zack plays with his basketball

b-Zack sleeps

c-Zack plays with his phone

d-Zack is out

3-When does Zack play basketball?

a-After classes

b-Before classes

c-When he does not have class

d-During the weekend

4-What color is the jersey that Zack gives to Mathieu?

a Red

b-Blue

c-Yellow

d-Orange

5-What clue tells Mathieu that people are playing in the field?

a-He hears people talking

b-He hears people laughing

c-He hears the rebounds of the ball

d-He hears footsteps

6-What are the names of the opponents of Zack and Mathieu?

7-Why can Mathieu and Zack join the game?

8-Why does Mathieu stop playing?

9-How does Mathieu feel after the match?

10-Does Mathieu plan to play basketball again? Why?

Chapter 4 – Bella

Fromage, frites, sandwich, bon sang. J'ai l'impression d'être un gamin à faire la même chose jour après jour. Je me suis dégoté un petit boulot à temps partiel deux mois après m'être installé en France, histoire de me faire un peu d'argent en parallèle de l'université. Ce n'est pas une tâche facile mais il faut bien commencer quelque part. Je travaille comme serveur dans un petit « fast-food » pas très loin de chez moi. Ma famille me manque, c'est donc surtout pour me distraire et oublier ma solitude.

Mais j'ai tant de choses à faire et pas mal de préoccupations pour le moment.

« Garnitures ? »

Ça fait juste deux cent fois que je demande ça depuis que j'ai ouvert la porte ce matin.

« Qu'est-ce que vous avez ? »

Le monsieur à ma fenêtre porte une chemise bleue, un téléphone dans une main et une tasse de café dans l'autre. Je ne sais pas comment il va se débrouiller pour tenir un sandwich aussi, mais c'est son problème, pas le mien. J'ai suffisamment de soucis de mon côté, je n'ai pas besoin de me rajouter ceux des autres.

« Il y a tout sur la pancarte à gauche. »

Je fais un signe de tête en direction du panneau pourtant très distinct avec de grandes lettres noires et blanches qui indique clairement toutes les garnitures que je propose.

« Voilà, ce sont les plus populaires.

– Vous avez quelque chose de plus sain ? »

Il est dans un fast-food et il veut quelque chose de sain.

La queue s'allonge et je peux voir des regards le mitrailler.

« Je prendrai juste un sandwich au poulet dans ce cas. »

Évidemment.

« C'est noté. Ça prendra quelques minutes. »

J'encaisse son argent et je me retourne vers les fourneaux pour en sortir deux gaufres presque brûlées. Ça bipait depuis qu'il avait commencé à chercher son portefeuille dans son sac bien trop grand.

Un autre jour. Un autre euro. Rien de mieux que de rentrer à la maison.

Il est tout juste dix-huit heures passées et je suis prêt à fermer boutique mais comme je n'ai pas encore vu Bella pour l'instant, je m'occupe en organisant les étagères. J'attends ma dose journalière de paradis. Bien entendu, Bella n'est pas son vrai nom. Je ne lui ai parlé qu'une fois et je ne lui ai pas demandé son prénom.

Et, réglée comme une horloge, la voilà qui passe dans un t-shirt blanc et un pantalon noir skinny. Ses cheveux bruns arrivent à ses épaules, sa petite frange est balayée par le vent. Me voilà à l'admirer.

Elle passe devant ma fenêtre tous les soirs de la semaine à dix-huit heures dix exactement. Jamais avant. Jamais après. Toujours à la même heure. Si je devais deviner, je dirais qu'elle habite dans le coin également.

La seule fois où Bella est venue à ma fenêtre, c'était il y a environ un mois. Il était trois heures de l'après-midi, un samedi. Elle était seule, portait un T-shirt des Oregon Ducks. J'étais stressé. J'ai remarqué son sourire insouciant.

Elle a peut-être dix-huit ou dix-neuf ans, plus jeune de quelques années par rapport à moi, mais j'ai l'impression d'être un vieux quand je regarde sa peau de porcelaine et ses yeux verts angéliques.

Alors, comme une brise, Bella passe devant ma fenêtre. Mon ego essaie de me convaincre qu'elle a lancé un regard dans ma direction, mais je sais que je rêve.

C'est l'heure de rentrer. Et hop, je ferme la boutique et je dis bonne soirée à mes collègues.

Cheese, fries, bread, oh my God. I feel like a kid doing the same thing day after day.

'Toppings?'

It's been just two hundred times since I opened the door this morning.

'What do you offer?'

The man at my window is wearing a blue shirt, a phone in one hand and a coffee mug in the other. I do not know how he's going to hold a sandwich too, but that's his problem, not mine. I have enough concerns on my side. I do not need to add some more.

'There is everything on the sign on the left.'

I nod in the direction of the very distinct panel with large black and white letters that clearly indicates all the toppings I propose.

'These are the most popular.'

'Do you have something healthier?'

He's in a fast food restaurant and he wants something that's healthy.

The line is getting longer and I can see all the dirty looks that are staring at him.

'I'll just take a chicken sandwich then.'

Obviously.

'Noted. It will take a few minutes.'

I cash his money and turn to the stove to get out two waffles that are almost burned. It started beeping when he was looking for his wallet in his big bag.

Another day. Another dollar. Nothing better than home.

It's just 6:00 pm and I'm ready to close, but since I have not seen Bella for now, I'm organizing my shelves once again and waiting for my daily dose of paradise. Bella is not her real name, of course, but since I only spoke to her once, I do not know her first name.

And, set like a clock, here she is in a white t-shirt and skinny black pants, her brown hair coming to her shoulders, with little bangs that the wind sweeps from time to time, and here I am, admiring her.

She walks by my window every night of the week at exactly six past ten. Never before. Never after. Always at the same time. If I had to guess, I would say she lives in the area as well.

The only time Bella came to my window was about a month ago. It was three o'clock in the afternoon, a Saturday, and she was alone, wearing an Oregon Ducks t-shirt. I had never seen her that close before. I was stressed. I noticed her carefree smile.

She may be eighteen or nineteen years old. A few years younger than me, but I feel like an old man when I look at her porcelain skin and angelic green eyes.

Does she like me? The only signs I noticed indicating that she wanted anything were those deep breaths she took to smell food's smell in the air every time she passed my window. I do not know why she does not stop more often, but it's none of my business.

Then, like a gust of wind, Bella passes in front of me, inspiring me deeply in passing. My ego tries to convince me that she has also looked in my direction, but I know I'm dreaming.

Résumé

Deux mois après son arrivée en France, Mathieu décide de travailler à temps partiel dans un petit snack pas très loin de chez lui. Il sert les commandes dans une petite fenêtre. Il n'y a rien de particulier qui attire son attention dans le coin, à part la jeune fille qui passe tous les jours devant l'endroit où il travaille. Il ne la connaît pas, mais la trouve particulièrement charmante. Pourtant il est encore occupé, donc il préfère suivre son train-train quotidien*.

Summary

Two months after his arrival in France, Mathieu decides to work part-time in a small snack bar not far from home. He serves the orders in a small window. There is nothing special around but he sees a girl who passes every day in front of the place where he works. He does not know her, but finds her particularly charming. Still he is busy so he prefers to follow his daily routine *.

Vocabulaire / Vocabulary

fromage - cheese

frites - fries

dégoté un petit boulot - got a job (informal)

à temps partiel - part-time

tâche facile - easy task

serveur - server

garnitures - toppings

préoccupations - concerns

solitude - loneliness

pancarte - sign

étagères - shelves

frange - bangs

angélique(s) - angelic

horloge - clock

peau de porcelaine - porcelain skin

odeur - smell

*Train-train quotidien** - literally means "daily train-train" which means something that you usually do, something you are used to do; it's an expression to call your daily routine.

Questions

1 - Depuis quand Mathieu travaille-t-il dans le fast-food ?

a. Deux semaines après son arrivée en France

b. Deux mois après son arrivée en France

c. Quatre mois après son arrivée en France

2 - Quel poste occupe-t-il dans le fast-food ?

a. Il est serveur.

b. Il est gérant.

c. Il est cuisinier.

3 - Mathieu travaille à temps partiel :

a. Vrai

b. Faux

4 - Qui est Bella ?

a. Une amie

b. Une fille qui passe souvent devant son travail

c. Une cliente

5 - A quelle heure Bella passe-t-elle devant le fast-food ?

a. 18 heures

b. 20 heures

c. 18 heures 10 minutes

6 - Que portait Bella ce jour-là ?

7 - Quel âge Mathieu pense-t-il que Bella a ?

8 - Est-ce que Bella passe tous les jours ?

9 - Est-ce que Bella est le vrai nom de la fille ?

10 - Est-ce que Mathieu a déjà parlé à Bella ? Et quand ?

Questions

1-Since when does Mathieu work in a fast food?

a-Two weeks after arriving in France

b-Two months after arriving in France

c-Four months after arriving in France

2-What position does he occupy in fast food?

a-He is a waiter

b-He is manager

c-He is a cook

3-Mathieu works part-time:

a-True

b-False

4-Who is Bella?

a-A friend

b-A girl who often goes to work

c-A client

5-What time does Bella pass in front of the fast food?

a-18 :00 pm

b-20 :00 pm

c-18 :10 pm

6- What was Bella wearing that day?

7-How old does Mathieu think Bella is?

8- Is Bella passing every day?

9-Is Bella the real name of the girl?

10-Has Mathieu ever talked to Bella? And when?

Réponses

1 - b

2 - a

3 - a

4 - b

5 - c

6 - Bella portait un t-shirt blanc et un pantalon noir skinny.

7 - Il pense juste qu'elle est plus jeune que lui.

8 - Oui, Bella passe tous les jours.

9 - Non, c'est un surnom que Mathieu lui a donné.

10 - Oui, une fois quand elle a acheté à manger dans le fast-food.

Answers

1-b

2-a

3-a

4-b

5-c

6- Bella was wearing a white t-shirt and skinny black pants.

7-He just thinks she's younger than him.

8- Yes, Bella passes by the front of his window every day.

9-No, it's a nickname Mathieu gave her.

10-Yes, once when she bought something in the fast food.

Chapter 5 – Une tarte aux pommes

J'ouvre les yeux au moins vingt secondes avant que le réveil ne sonne. Je m'appelle Henri et j'ai cinquante ans. J'ai trois enfants, Marie, Mathieu et Quentin, des enfants bien intelligents et dont je suis fier. Les deux aînés sont partis continuer leurs études universitaires à l'étranger. Marie est en Allemagne et Mathieu en France. Pour ce qui est de Quentin, le petit dernier, nous ne savons pas ce qu'il projette de faire, mais pour le moment il est parti vivre en colocation avec un de ses amis et nous le voyons encore pendant les weekends, ou quand il n'a pas cours. C'est fou ce que les enfants grandissent vite, le temps file à toute allure.

Ma femme Zoé dort encore. Sans trop tarder, je me lève et je vais dans la salle de bain me laver le visage pour effacer les traces de l'oreiller. Je porte un débardeur et un short, il est six heures du matin. Je prends la serviette suspendue sous le miroir et je m'essuie le visage avec elle.

Je me change avant de me diriger vers la cuisine pour prendre mon petit déjeuner. J'entends Zoé se lever.

« Tu es bien matinal aujourd'hui.

– Oh, je n'avais plus sommeil, dis-je en ouvrant le frigo.

– Il y a des céréales aux fruits rouges si ça te dis, chéri.

– Mhhh, non c'est bon, je vais juste manger des biscottes. Fais-nous du café plutôt.

– Oui, chef, dit-elle en sautillant.

– Tu n'as toujours pas de nouvelles des enfants ?

– Non.

– Marie ? Mathieu ? Et Quentin ?

– Ils sont sûrement occupés. Quentin a appelé hier soir quand tu étais encore au travail. Il passera dimanche, il veut nous présenter sa petite copine, Clémence.

– Eh bien, comme je le pensais, le temps passe vite. Et dire qu'il y a un an, on déposait Mathieu à l'aéroport et voilà que Quentin a une petite copine ! dis-je en riant.

– Nous avons bien fait de prendre cet appartement. A nous deux, la maison était bien trop grande. En plus, notre portier Marcello est extrêmement sympathique.

– Oui, c'est sûr. Mais il se fait vieux, il devrait partir à la retraite pour enfin pouvoir se reposer.

– Il n'a pas de famille apparemment. Et puis son travail ne le fatigue pas tant que ça je pense. »

Le téléphone sonne. Zoé s'empresse de regarder le nom affiché sur l'écran. Déçue, elle le tend à Henri : c'est un de ses amis qui l'appelle.

« Bon, je vais faire une tarte, je sors faire quelques emplettes pour acheter les ingrédients.

– Moi aussi je veux sortir faire un tour.

– Allons-y ensemble alors.

– D'accord. Préparons-nous alors », dis-je.

Nous avons eu un déjeuner calme. C'était délicieux, j'adore les lasagnes, surtout avec des champignons. En début d'après-midi, on a regardé quelques feuilletons. Puis j'ai enfilé mes lunettes pour lire les journaux pendant qu'elle continuait à regarder ses séries.

« Bon, je vais aller faire ma tarte. Je n'ai pas envie de commencer trop tard, je serai fatiguée ensuite et je n'aime pas remettre à demain, dit-elle en se levant.

– Moi je pense faire une petite sieste.

– Est-ce que tu ne serais pas mieux dans le lit ?

– Oh que non, le canapé est bien meilleur, crois-moi.

– Si tu le dis. »

Je ne sais plus quelle heure il est quand j'ouvre les yeux. Il commence à faire nuit. Je me lève et vais vers la cuisine. Ça sent le gâteau. Zoé est justement en train de sortir la tarte du four. Elle en profite pour humer la douce odeur de tarte sortant du four.

« Et voilà, je n'ai pas perdu la main ! dit-elle en souriant comme une enfant.

– Ça a l'air bon.

– C'est l'odeur qui t'a réveillé ? Tu semblais dormir tellement bien que je n'ai pas osé te réveiller.

– Je me suis assoupi un instant et puis hop ! »

Je m'assieds et la regarde découper deux morceaux de la tarte.

« Tu veux qu'on l'appelle ?

– Qui donc ?

– Mathieu voyons. Je sais que c'est son anniversaire et que c'est pour ça que tu as fais cette tarte. Une tarte aux pommes, hein ? C'est ce qui m'a mis la puce à l'oreille.

– C'est sa préférée… Il doit être occupé, je ne veux pas le déranger.

– Mais non, c'est vendredi, il doit sûrement avoir un peu de temps. Et puis on ne le dérangera pas longtemps. On va juste lui souhaiter un joyeux anniversaire ! dis-je en déverrouillant mon smartphone. En plus il est connecté ! ajoutais-je.

– Vraiment ? Appelle-le alors ! », dit-elle en se rapprochant de moi.

Ça bipe un moment, il ne décroche pas. On essaye une seconde fois, rien.

On attend cinq minutes avant de retenter, au cas où il serait sorti un instant, et on rappelle. Cette fois, il décroche.

« Allô ? Bonjour papa.

– Bonjour fiston, ça va ? On t'appelle juste pour…

– Joyeux anniversaire chééééerii ! », s'empresse Zoé par-dessus mon épaule gauche.

J'entends Mathieu rire, je ris à mon tour.

« Oui, voilà, joyeux anniversaire fiston, c'est pour te dire que nous t'aimons et que nous pensons à toi.

– Tu nous manques !

– Vous me manquez aussi… Et merci de ne pas avoir oublié. Et désolé de ne pas vous avoir appelé souvent.

– Ce n'est rien, tu dois être occupé.

– Appelle-nous quand tu as le temps, OK ?

– Ça marche !

– On a fait une tarte aux pommes, tu t'en rappelles ? C'est ta préférée.

– Mhhhh, oui oui. Ça fait longtemps que je n'en ai pas mangé. Tiens je vais m'en acheter après.

– Sinon, ça va ?

– Oui, mais je dois vous laisser. Je vais sortir avec des amis.

– Pas de souci, vas-y. Nous sommes heureux de t'avoir eu au téléphone aujourd'hui ! dis-je.

– Moi aussi mes parents chéris ! Ah, et Marie m'a appelé, elle m'a dit qu'elle pourrait sûrement venir me voir d'ici peu. Elle n'a encore rien dit, mais vous la connaissez avec ses mystères.

– Quelle bonne nouvelle, appelez-nous quand vous serez ensemble, lança Zoé.

– Oui, maman ! Promis ! Bises !

– Bisous !

– Au revoir fiston. »

Quand il a raccroché, Zoé a pris un morceau de tarte et me l'a tendu. C'est bon, je suis heureux. On a eu notre fils au téléphone et on a pu lui souhaiter un joyeux anniversaire.

I open my eyes at least 20 seconds before the alarm rings. My name is Henri and I'm 50 years old. I have three children, Marie, Mathieu and Quentin, very intelligent children, of whom I am proud. The two elders left to continue their college studies abroad. Marie is in Germany and Mathieu in France. As for Quentin, the youngest, we do not know what he's planning to do, but for the moment he's gone off to live with a friend of his and we see him on weekends or when he's not at his classes. It's crazy how children grow up fast, time flies.

Zoe still sleeps. Without too much delay I get up and go to the bathroom to wash my face to remove the traces of the pillow. I wear a tank top and a shirt ; it is 6am in the morning. I find the towel under the mirror and I wipe my face with it.

I change before heading to the kitchen for breakfast. I hear Zoé getting up.

'You are early today.'

'Oh, I was no longer sleepy,' I say opening the fridge.

'We have red fruit cereals if you want, darling.'

'Mhhh, no it's good, I'm just going to eat crackers. Make us some coffee instead.'

'Yes, sir.' She said, hopping.

'You still have no news from the children?'

'No.'

'Marie? Mathieu, and Quentin?'

'They are probably busy. Quentin called last night when you were still at work. He will come on Sunday, he wants to introduce his girlfriend, Clemence.'

'Well, as I said time flies. Thinking that just a year ago we were dropping off Mathieu at the airport, and now Quentin has a girlfriend!"l I said with a little chuckle.

'We did well by taking this apartment, the house was way too big just for the two of us. Moreover, we have a friendly doorman.''

Yes, but Marcello is getting old, he has to rest and retire.'

'But he does not have a family, and it seems like his work is not so much tiring.'

The phone rings. Zoé hastens to see the name displayed on the screen. Disappointed she hands it to me, it is one of my friends calling.

'Good, I'm going to make a pie. I will go out shopping to buy the ingredients.'

'I'm going out for a walk.'

'We will go together then.'

'Okay. Let's get ready,' I said.

We had a quiet lunch, it was delicious, I really like lasagna, especially with mushrooms. In the early afternoon we watched a few soap operas and she continued watching her shows while I put on my glasses to read the newspapers.

'Good, I'll go make my pie. I do not want to start too late, I will be tired and I do not want to postpone it until tomorrow.' She said, standing up.

'Yes, I'm going to take a nap.'

'Wouldn't it better to sleep on the bed?'

'Oh no, the sofa is better, believe me.'

'If you say so.'

I do not know what time it is when I open my eyes ; it is getting dark. I get up and go to the kitchen. It smells like pie, Zoe is just taking out the pie from the oven. She seizes the opportunity to smell the odor that the pie gives off.

'And here, I did not lose the knack!' she said, smiling like a child.

'It looks good.'

'Is it the smell that woke you up? You seemed to sleep so well that I did not dare to wake you up.'

'I fell asleep for a moment and then hop!'

I sat down and watched her cut out two pieces of the pie.

'Do you want to make a call?'

'Who?'

'Mathieu. I know it's his birthday and that's why you made this pie. An apple pie, huh?' That's what set me thinking she would like to call him.

'It's his favorite ... He must be busy, I do not want to disturb him.'

'But no, it's Friday, he must surely have some time. And then we will not disturb him for a long time. We're just going to wish him a happy birthday!' I say unlocking my smartphone.

'In addition he is connected!' I added.

'Really? Call him then!' she said, coming closer to me.

It beeps for a moment, he does not pick up. We try a second time, nothing.

We wait five minutes before retrying in case it takes a moment and we call back. This time he picks up.

'Allo? Hello, Dad.'

'Hello son, how are you? We call you for...'

' Happy birthday honeeeeeey.' says Zoé over my left shoulder. I hear Mathieu laughing, I laugh in turn.

'Yes, voilà, happy birthday son, we love you.'

'We miss you!'

'I miss you too... And thank you for not having forgotten. And sorry for not calling you often.'

'It's nothing, you must be busy.'

'Well call us when you have time. OK?'

'I'll do it !'

'We did an apple pie, remember? It's your favorite.'

'Mhhhh, yes yes. I have not eaten it for a long time. Maybe I'll buy some after.'

'Then, how are you doing?'

'Good, but I have to leave. I am going out with friends.'

'No worries, go ahead. We are happy we could talk to you today !'

'So did I, my dear parents! Ah, and Marie called me, she told me she could probably come and see me. She has not said anything yet but, you know, her and her mysteries.'

'That's good news, call us then,' said Zoé.

'Yes mom! Promised! Hugs!'

'Kisses!'

'-See you, son.'

When he hung up Zoe took a piece of pie and handed it to me. 'It's good, I'm happy, we had our son on the phone and we could wish him a happy birthday.'

Sommaire

Henri a 50 ans. Il habite avec sa femme Zoé dans un petit appartement après que ses enfants soient tous partis. Ce jour là, il se lève à 6h du matin. C'est un jour comme les autres, il se douche et descend pour prendre son petit déjeuner. Zoé le rejoint, ils passent une journée comme les autres et Zoé décide de faire une tarte aux pommes, ce qui surprend Henri, étant donné qu'elle a arrêté d'en faire depuis trois ans. En effet, Henri se doute qu'elle fait cette tarte à l'occasion de l'anniversaire de leur fils Mathieu. Ils réussissent à l'avoir au téléphone et peuvent lui souhaiter un joyeux anniversaire comme il faut.

Summary

Henri is 50 years old. He lives with his wife, Zoe, in a small apartment after his children are all gone. That day, he gets up at 6 am. It is a day like the others, he showers and goes down to have breakfast. Zoe joins him. They spend an ordinary day and Zoe decides to make an apple pie, which surprises Henri since it has been 3 years that she stopped doing it. Indeed, Henri suspected that the reason she had made this pie was for the occasion of the birthday of their son Mathieu. They get him on the phone and wish him a happy birthday.

Vocabulaire / Vocabulary

secondes - seconds

réveil - alarm

fier - proud

aînés - elders

coloc' – shared appartment

c'est fou - it's crazy

serviette - towel

miroir - mirror

la cuisine - kitchen

petit déjeuner - breakfast

salle de bain - bathroom

oreiller - pillow

débardeur - tank top

short - shorts

sommeil - sleep

céréales - cereal

dimanche - Sunday

sympathique - nice

retraite - retirement

écran - screen

tarte aux pommes - apple pie

champignons - mushrooms

une sieste - a nap

morceau - piece

canapé - sofa

joyeux anniversaire – happy birthday

Questions

1 - Comment s'appelle le monsieur de l'histoire ?

a. Henri

b. François

c. Carl

d. Damien

2 - Qui est Zoé ?

a. La mère d'Henri

b. La sœur d'Henri

c. La femme d'Henri

d. La cousine d'Henri

3 - Quel âge a Henri ?

a. Henri a 60 ans.

b. Henri a 45 ans.

c. Henri a 52 ans.

d. Henri a 50 ans.

4 - Combien d'enfants a Henri ?

a. Henri a trois enfants.

b. Henri n'a pas d'enfant.

c. Henri a deux enfants.

d. Henri a six enfants.

5 - Que porte Henri ?

a. Une chemise et un jean

b. Un débardeur et un short

c. Un capuchon et un short

d. Un pyjama satin

6 - Qu'est-ce qu'Henri veut manger au petit déjeuner ?

7 – Quelle tarte veut préparer Zoé ?

8 - Qu'est-ce qu'Henri et Zoé ont mangé pour le déjeuner ?

9 - Qui a appelé sur le portable d'Henri ?

10 - Pourquoi Zoé a-t-elle fait une tarte aux pommes ?

Questions

1-What is the name of the gentleman of the story?

a- Henri

b-Francois

c-Carl

d-Damien

2-Who is Zoe?

a-Henri's mother

b-Henri's sister

c-Henri's wife

d-Henri's cousin

3-How old is Henri?

a-Henri is 60 years old

b-Henri is 45 years old

c-Henri is 52 years old

d-Henri is 50 years old

4-How many children does Henri have?

a-Henri has three children

b-Henri does not have any children

c-Henri has two children

d-Henri has six children

5-What's Henri wearing?

a- a shirt and jeans

b-tank top and shorts

c-a hood and shorts

d-satin pajamas

6-What does Henri want to eat for breakfast?

7-What tart does Zoe want to cook?

8-What did Henri and Zoe eat for lunch?

9-Who called on Messenger on Henri's laptop?

10-Why did Zoé make an apple pie?

Réponses

1 - a

2 - c

3 - d

4 - a

5 - b

6 - Henri veut des biscottes et du café.

7 - Zoé veut faire une tarte aux pommes.

8 - Henri et Zoé ont mangé des lasagnes aux champignons pour le déjeuner.

9 - C'est un ami d'Henri qui l'a appelé.

10 - Zoé a fait une tarte aux pommes parce que c'est l'anniversaire de Mathieu aujourd'hui.

Answers

1-a

2-c

3-d

4-a

5-b

6-Henry wants rusks and coffee.

7-Zoe wants to prepare an apple pie.

8-Henri and Zoé ate mushroom lasagna during lunch.

9-It's a friend of Henri who called on Messenger.

10-Zoe made an apple pie because it's Mathieu's birthday today.

Chapter 6 – L'anniversaire de Zack

Zack et moi sommes devenus de très bons amis. Cela va faire un an que je suis arrivé à Toulouse et depuis, je suis plus heureux que jamais. Bien sûr ma vie n'a rien d'extraordinaire, mais j'aime ce que je suis devenu. Nous venons de clôturer la période des examens et nous sommes maintenant en vacances.

Mes cheveux sont plus longs, je peux les attacher maintenant. Je ne suis plus aussi maigre qu'avant, vu que je fais un peu plus de sport et que je mange mieux. Nous sommes aujourd'hui le quatre juillet et Zack fête ses vingt-et-un ans. Il veut organiser une petite fête entre amis. J'ai pu faire la connaissance de beaucoup de ses amis depuis et ils sont tous très sympas.

« Alors, tu comptes faire quoi aujourd'hui ? je lui demande.

– Mhhh, finalement, il n'y aura pas de fête.

– Pourquoi ça ? Tu en parles tous les jours depuis une semaine.

– Oui, mais finalement je n'ai pas besoin d'une grosse fête, juste une sortie sympa entre amis. Et juste les amis proches. Oui, tu *es* invité.

– Ça me touche, je ne sais pas quoi dire… merci mec ! »

Je lui fais une petite tape sur l'épaule.

Honnêtement, ça m'a touché. Je n'ai jamais eu beaucoup d'amis et savoir que Zack me considère comme un ami proche me fait très plaisir.

« Et j'ai une autre surprise...

– Mais c'est mon anniversaire aujourd'hui ou le tien ? Qu'est-ce que c'est ?

– C'est une surprise, je te dis. Tu verras là-bas.

– Mais où est-ce qu'on va ?

– Il y a un petit resto sympa en ville. Jean passera nous prendre en début de soirée. »

Jean est un ami d'enfance de Zack. Il vit seul et va à l'université à Paris. Il est passé à Toulouse exprès pour l'anniversaire de Zack et dort à l'hôtel.

Je me dirige vers le canapé et m'y allonge. Je vais juste fermer les yeux une minute avant de me préparer à sortir.

Quand je réouvre les yeux, le soleil était en train de se coucher. Je farfouille pour trouver mon téléphone, le trouvant coincé sous un oreiller du canapé.

Dix neuf heures.

« Oh, non! »

Je me lève. Mon corps protestait, j'étais encore endormi.

Je me suis préparé en moins de dix minutes : juste le temps d'arranger mes cheveux, de passer de l'eau fraîche sur mon visage et de me changer. Je regarde ma montre pour voir l'heure. Zack n'est toujours pas là... ou est-ce moi qui ai mal compris l'heure à laquelle Jean doit passer ?

A peine cette réflexion faite, le voilà qui entre.

« Tu es déjà prêt ? Tu dormais comme un bébé, je n'ai pas osé te réveiller. Jean est en route, il sera là dans dix minutes.

– Et ma surprise ? Tu vas me le dire maintenant ?

– Patience, patience ! »

Il me fit un clin d'œil.

Nous nous sommes garés dans le parking d'un restaurant chinois assez chic. Nous étions cinq, dont Zack et sa copine Léa, Jean et sa petite amie Carole, et moi. Jean et Carole étaient des camarades de classe de Zack au lycée. Ils sortent ensemble depuis la classe de terminale. Nous étions tous là, alors qu'attendions-nous ?

« OK, on attend quoi maintenant ? Nous sommes tous là, non ? Est-ce qu'on attend encore quelqu'un ? »

Zack regarda sa montre et fronça les sourcils.

« Eh bien, soit elle est en retard, soit elle m'a fait faux bond, dit-il nerveusement.

– De qui parles-tu ? » demandai-je

Jean et Léa se regardaient. Je pouvais voir les sourires qu'ils cachaient maladroitement sur leurs visages. Qu'est-ce qu'ils mijotaient ?

Zack regarde derrière moi, vers la rue, et lâcha un soupir de soulagement.

« Voilà ta surprise qui arrive ! » dit-il tout en gloussant.

J'ai failli m'esclaffer en me retournant et en voyant de loin la petite brune avec une robe fleurie et des escarpins marrons. C'était Bella.

« Je n'arrive pas à croire que tu l'ai invité ! dis-je en me retournant vers lui.

– Hahaha ! Depuis le temps que tu me parles d'elle, j'ai décidé de lui parler et de lui proposer de nous rejoinder ce soir.

– Et elle a accepté ?

– Bien sûr que non ! Au début en tout cas. J'ai insister un peu avant qu'elle n'accepte. Une vraie antisociale ! Vous allez très bien ensemble, dit-il en rigolant.

– J'y crois pas ! T'as intérêt à ce qu'elle ne se fiche pas de moi.

– Mais non, tais-toi, elle arrive.

– Bonsoir, je suis en retard, désolée, dit-elle.

– Quelles bonnes manières ! », je réplique.

Il m'a fallu quelques secondes avant de me rendre compte de ce que je venais de dire. Elle me foudroyait du regard.

« Oh, je me suis excusé, monsieur fast-food. »

J'étais à la fois choqué et heureux. Elle me reconnaissait. J'aurais préféré qu'elle se souvienne de moi en dehors de mon job au fast-food, mais quand même !

« Désolé, il n'a pas l'habitude de parler à des filles !

– Mais…

– Ne l'écoute pas, merci d'être venue.

– Je n'avais pas vraiment le choix. Je ne veux surtout pas gâcher ta fête. »

Pendant que notre groupe rentrait dans le restaurant, moi et Bella étions derrière, marchant côte à côte sans parler.

« Au fait, Zack m'a dit que tu me surnommais Bella. », lança-t-elle.

Cet imbécile, je vais le tuer. 1 lui a sûrement tout raconté. Je restais silencieux. Elle s'est tournée vers moi, elle était maquillée.

« Bella est flatteur comme surnom, mais je m'appelle Laura. »

Je lui tendis la main.

« Enchanté, Laura. »

Et elle serra ma main sans rien dire.

Zack and I became very good friends. It will be soon be a year since I arrived in Toulouse and I am happier than ever. Of course my life is not extraordinary, but I like what I have become. We just finished the exam periods and we are now on holidays.

I let my hair grow a little bit so I can tie it up. I'm not as skinny as I used to be because I do more exercise than before and I eat healthier. It's July 4th and Zack is turning 21 today. He wants to throw party for his birthday. I've met a lot of his friends and they are all nice.

'So, what are you going to do today?' I asked.

'Mhhh, there will be no party.'

'What, why? You've been talking about it for days.'

'Yes but I do not want a big party anymore, just a nice evening out with friends. Just close friends. And yes, you are invited.'

'It's really nice of you, I do not know what to say ... thanks, dude!' I give him a pat on the shoulder.

Honestly, I appreciated this, I never had many friends and to know that Zack considers me a close friend represented something to me. I am happy.

'And I have another surprise for you.'

'Is this my birthday or yours? What is it?'

'I told you it's a surprise. You will see there.'

'But where are we going?'

'There is a nice little restaurant in town. Jean will take us there in the early evening.'

Jean is a childhood friend of Zack's. He lives alone and goes to the University of Paris. He went to Toulouse especially for Zack's birthday, he sleeps at the hotel.

I laid down on the couch. I just wanted to close my eyes for a minute before getting ready to go out.

When I opened my eyes again, it was getting dark. I looked around for my phone, finding it stuck under a pillow.

7pm.

"Oh, no," I said.

I'm standing up. My body protested, I still fell asleep.

I prepared myself in ten minutes, just enough time to arrange my hair, put cool water on my face and change. I looked up the time on my watch. Zack was still not there… did I misunderstand the time Jean was supposed to come pick us up?

While thinking about it, Zach comes in.

'Are you ready? You slept like a baby, I did not want to wake you up. Jean is on his way he will be there in ten minutes.'

'What about my surprise? Are you going to tell me now?'

'Patience, patience!'

He winked at me.

We parked in the car park of a chic Chinese restaurant. There were five of us including Zack and his girlfriend Lea, Jean and his girlfriend Carole and me. Jean and Carole were Zack's classmates in high school. They were dating since senior year. We were all there, so what were we waiting for?

'Ok, what are we doing now? We are all here, right? Or are we still waiting for someone?'

Zack looked at his watch and frowned.

-Well, she's either late or failed me.' he said nervously.

'Who are you talking about ?' I asked.

Jean and Leah were looking at each other, I could see the smiles they clumsily hid on their faces. What was happening?

Zack looks behind me towards the street and lets out a sigh of relief.

'Here is your surprise,' he said to me while giggling.

I turned around and almost laughed while seeing the little brunette with a flowery dress and brown pumps from afar. It was Bella.

'I can not believe you invited her to your birthday!' I say, turning to him.

'Hahaha! Since you told to me about her I decided to meet her and ask her to come tonight.'

'And she accepted?'

'Of course not at first. I had to insist a little before she accepted. A real antisocial! You will get along very well together,' he said laughing.

'I can't believe it ! I hope for you she will not make fun of me.'

'Shut up, she's coming.'

'Good evening, I'm late, sorry,' she says.

'What good manners!' I said.

It took me a few seconds to realize what I had just said as she glared at me.

'Oh, I just apologized, Mr. Fast Food.'

I was both shocked and happy. She knew me. I wish she remembered me outside of my job at a fast food, but still, she knew me!

'Sorry, he's not used to talk to girls!'

'But…'

'Do not listen to him, thank you for coming.'

'I did not really have a choice. I did not want to ruin your party.'

As our group entered the restaurant, Bella and I were walking behind, side by side, without speaking.

'Actually, Zack told me that you nicknamed me Bella,' she said.

This idiot, I'm going to kill him. He probably told her everything. I stayed silent. She turned to me. She was wearing makeup.

'Bella is flattering as a nickname but my name is Laura.'

I held out my hand.

'Nice to meet you, Laura.'

And she squeezed my hand without saying anything.

Résumé

Ça va faire un an que Mathieu est en France et depuis, lui et Zack sont devenus inséparables. Aujourd'hui, c'est l'anniversaire de Zack, et ce dernier veut faire une petite fête à l'occasion de ses vingt-et-un ans. Mathieu est touché quand Zack lui dit qu'il n'invite que ses amis proches et que Mathieu est invité à sa fête. Il lui annonce aussi qu'il y aura une surprise pour lui à cette fête. Ils partent pour le restaurant en début de soirée et Jean, un ami de Zack, passe les prendre chez eux. Arrivés à destination, ils attendent encore dehors et Mathieu se demande se qu'il se passe lorsqu'il voit arriver Bella, la fille dont il est amoureux. Surpris, il est sous le choc, c'est une bien bonne surprise !

Summary

It's been a year since Mathieu was in France and since then, he and Zack have become inseparable. Today is Zack's birthday and he wants to have a little party on the occasion of his 21 years. Mathieu appreciates a lot that Zack tells him that he only invites his close friends and that Mathieu is invited to his party. He also announces that there will be a surprise for him at this party. They leave for the restaurant in the early evening and Jean, a friend of Zack, picked them up from their place. Having arrived at their destination, they are still waiting outside and Mathieu wonders what happens when he sees Bella, the girl he is in love with. Surprised, he is shocked, it's a very good surprise!

Vocabulaire / Vocabulary

très bons amis - very good friends

clôturer - to end/to close/to finish

périodes d'examens - exams period

faire la connaissance de - to get to know

sortie - going out

anniversaire - birthday

ami d'enfance - childhood friend

coucher de soleil - sunset

montre - watch

réflexion - reflection

restaurant chinois - Chinese restaurant

camarades de classe - classmates

faire faux bond – to welsh / to let sb down

maladroitement – awkwardly/clumsily

surnommer - to give someone a nickname

flatteur - flattering

Questions

1 - Combien de temps Mathieu reste-il en France ?

a. Un an

b. Deux ans

c. Trois mois

d. Quelques semaines

2 - Quelle est la date de l'anniversaire de Zack ?

a. 24 avril

b. 21 juillet

c. 14 juillet

d. 4 juillet

3 - Quel âge a Zack ?

a. Zack a dix-neuf ans.

b. Zack a vingt-et-un ans.

c. Zack a trente ans.

d. Zack a vingt-deux ans.

4 - Où vont-ils aller pour l'anniversaire de Zack ?

a. Dans un bar

b. Dans une boîte de nuit

c. Au cinéma

d. Au restaurant

5 - Qui est Jean ?

a. Jean est l'ami d'enfance de Zack.

b. Jean est le colocataire de Zack.

c. Jean est le cousin de Zack.

d. Jean est le père de Zack.

6 - Qui va passer les chercher en voiture en début de soirée ?

7 - Qui est invité à la sortie de Zack ?

8 - Qui est Carole ?

9 - Dans quel genre de restaurant vont Mathieu et ses amis ?

10 - Qui est l'invitée surprise de Zack ?

Questions

1-How long does Mathieu stay in France?

a-One year

b-Two years

c-Three months

a few weeks

2-What is the date of Zack's birthday?

a-24th of April

b-21 July

July 14th

d-4 July

3-How old is Zack?

a-Zack is 19 years old

b-Zack is 21 years old

c-Zack is 30 years old

d-Zack is 22 years old

4-Where will they go for Zack's birthday?

a-In a bar

b-In a nightclub

c-To the cinema

d- to the restaurant

5-Who is Jean?

a-Jean is Zack's childhood friend

b-Jean is the roommate of Zack

c-Jean is Zack's cousin

d-Jean is Zack's father

6-Who will pick them up by car in the early evening?

7-Who are invited to the party of Zack?

8-Who is Carole?

9-In what kind of restaurant are Mathieu and his friends going?

10-Who is Zack's surprise guest?

Réponses

1 - a

2 - d

3 - b

4 - d

5 - a

6 - C'est Jean qui passe les prendre en voiture en début de soirée.

7 - Seuls les amis proches de Zack sont invités à son anniversaire.

8 - Carole est la petite amie de Jean, et une amie de Zack.

9 - Mathieu et ses amis vont dans un restaurant chinois.

10 - L'invitée surprise de Zack est Bella.

Answers

1-a

2d

3-b

4-d

5-a

6-It's Jean who is picking them up in the early evening.

7-Only friends close to Zack are invited to his birthday.

8-Carole is Jean's girlfriend and a friend of Zack.

9-Mathieu and his friends go to a Chinese restaurant.

10-The surprise guest of Zack is Bella.

Chapter 7 – Une panne de voiture

Vers dix heures, je quitte le travail et je m'arrête devant l'appartement de Laura. Elle ne vit qu'à quelques pâtés de maisons de chez moi. Ce n'était pas difficile de trouver. Elle se tient sur le trottoir, vêtue d'un jean et d'un t-shirt. Ses cheveux sont tirés en queue de cheval. Cette fois-ci, elle ne porte pas de maquillage. Je me rends compte qu'elle a des taches de rousseur, comme moi. C'est mignon.

« Tu es en retard. », me dit-elle en ouvrant la porte passager. Elle affiche une mine renfrognée.

« Juste de quelques minutes, dis-je.

– Quelles bonnes manières! », dit-elle. C'est exactement ce que je lui avais dit la première fois que nous nous étions rencontrés. Je lui souris.

« Touché. », dis-je. Elle entre dans la voiture et met sa ceinture.

Nous sommes silencieux pendant un moment, avec seulement la radio pour briser le silence. La voix féminine du GPS interrompt la chanson de temps en temps.

« Qu'est-ce que tu fais dans la vie ? je lui demande finalement.

– Je suis juriste, étudiante pour le moment. », répond-t-elle.

J'hoche la tête. Elle ressemble plutôt au type qui préfère travailler avec des nombres.

« Et toi ? », demande-t-elle.

Je jette un coup d'œil dans le rétroviseur et change de voie. La voiture fait un bruit de étrange, je fronce les sourcils en regardant sur le tableau de bord.

« Je suis en communication. », dis-je.

Elle hausse les épaules sans réponse. Nous sommes à un feu rouge.

La feu passe au vert, je redémarre la voiture. Il faut un moment pour qu'elle se lance, je fronce d'autant plus les sourcils. Je retente une deuxième fois, au cas où. La voiture vrombit, le moteur coupe pendant une seconde avant de rugir.

« Woah. », dis-je. Ça recommence. Le volant frémit dans mes mains. Un autre bruit sourd et la voiture est foutue. Je tourne les roues et la guide sur le bord de la route. Je m'arrête lentement.

« Qu'est-ce qui ne va pas ? interroge Laura.

– Je ne sais pas. Tire sur le levier du capot, tu veux bien ? C'est en dessous de la boîte à gants. »

Laura se penche en avant. Je sors de la voiture et j'entends le capot s'ouvrir lorsqu'elle trouve le levier. J'ouvre le capot et je regarde l'état du moteur.

« Tu vois quelque chose? », demande-t-elle en sortant de la voiture.

Je secoue la tête.

« Je ne connais que les bases. Je vais devoir appeler quelqu'un. »

Elle lève les yeux au ciel.

« Fantastique. », dit-elle avec sarcasme. Je sors mon téléphone et je téléphone aux services d'urgence.

Laura s'appuie contre la voiture. Je referme le capot et la rejoins. Nous regardons les voitures passer devant nous sans vraiment les regarder. Je sors de ma poche un paquet de cigarettes et j'en allume une.

Laura fronce les sourcils.

« Tu fumes ? »

« De temps en temps. Quand les choses sont stressantes. Quand je m'ennuie. Ou quand ça me dit. »

J'inhale profondément. La fumée remplit mes poumons. Je m'éloigne de Laura pour expirer.

« Crois-tu au mariage, Mathieu ? », me demande-t-elle tout d'un coup.

Je suis un peu surpris par sa question.

« Eh bien… Je pense que le mariage cause beaucoup de problèmes. Des problèmes qui auraient pu rester loin. La vie de couple est géniale, bien sûr, mais le mariage ? Je ne sais pas. »

Je lui lance un clin d'œil. Ce n'est pas du tout la personne que j'ai rencontré à l'anniversaire de Zack. Celle-ci est douce, gentille et réfléchie. OK, elle pense beaucoup. Mais elle n'est pas agaçante du tout.

« Pourquoi ne crois-tu pas au mariage ? », demande-t-elle.

Je hausse les épaules et reprends ma cigarette. J'expire la fumée et fais tomber la cendre.

« Je ne sais pas. Je pense que je croirai au marriage le jour où je rencontrerai quelqu'un qui en vaut la peine, avec qui je voudrais passer ma vie. Je n'ai pas encore trouvé cette personne, tu vois ? »

I took off from work and stopped in front of Laura's apartment around 10pm. She lived only a few blocks away from my house. It wasn't hard to find at all. She stood on the sidewalk, dressed in jeans and a t-shirt. Her hair was pulled back in a ponytail. She was not wearing makeup this time. I noticed she had freckles, just like me. I find it cute.

"You're late," she said while opening the passenger door. She looked grumpy.

"Only of a couple of minutes," I said.

"What good manners!" she said. It was exactly what I'd told her the first time I've met her. I grinned at her.

"*Touché*," I answered. She got into the car and put her seatbelt on.

We drove in silence for a while, with just the radio to break the silence. The female voice on the GPS was the interrupting the tune every now and then.

"So, what do you do?" I finally asked.

"I'm a lawyer, still studying," she said.

I nodded. She looked like the type that would rather work with numbers.

"What about you?" she asked.

I glanced in the rearview mirror and changed lanes for the upcoming turn. The car made a scraping sound and I frowned, looking confused at the dashboard.

"I'm studying communications," I said.

The car spluttered and the engine cut for a second before roaring.

"Woah," I said. Not again. The steering wheel shuddered in my hands. One more muffled sound and the car died. I turned the wheel and pulled onto the emergency lane of the road while the car still rolled. I stopped the car slowly.

"What's wrong?" Laura asked.

"I don't know. Could you please pull the lever for the hood? It's below the glove compartment."

Laura leaned forward. I got out of the car and heard the hood click open as she found the lever. I opened the hood and looked at the engine.

"Can you see anything?" Laura asked, getting out of the car too.

I shook my head. "I only know the basics. I'm going to have to call someone."

Laura rolled her eyes and turned around.

"This is just *fantastic*," she said sarcastically. I pulled out my phone and dialed emergency services.

Laura leaned against the car. I closed the hood again and joined her. We watched cars passing by without really watching anything. I fished in my pocket for a pack of cigarettes and lit one up.

Laura frowned at me. "Do you smoke?"

I shrugged. "Here and there. When things are stressful. Or if I'm bored. Or if I feel like it." I inhaled deeply. Smoke filled my lungs. I exhaled away from Laura.

"Do you believe in marriage, Mathieu?" she asked out of the blue.

I am surprised by her question.

"Well… I believe marriage brings a lot of problems. Problems that could have been avoided. Being in a relationship is great, of course, but marriage? I don't know about that."

I wink at her. She wasn't the girl I'd met at Zach's party at all. She was sweet, kind and thoughtful. Sure, she overthinks stuff. But she doesn't sound annoying at all.

"Why don't you believe in marriage?" she asked.

I shrugged, pulling on my cigarette again. I blew out the smoke and tapped off the ash.

"I don't know. I guess I'll believe in it one I'll meet someone who's really worth it, someone I would want to spend the rest of my life with. I haven't found anyone like that yet, you see?"

Sommaire

Mathieu a pu rencontrer Laura à l'anniversaire de son ami Zack, et depuis, il a réussi à avoir un rendez-vous avec elle. Lorsqu'il vient la chercher chez elle après le travail, elle semble différente de la fille qu'il a rencontrée à la fête : elle est moins maquillée et a un tout autre caractère. Lorsqu'ils discutent dans la voiture, le moteur commence à émettre d'étranges bruits ; après un moment, ils tombent en panne. Quelle poisse pour un premier rendez-vous ! Mais finalement, bien que le rendez-vous soit gâché, Mathieu a l'occasion de parler avec Laura et d'en apprendre plus sur elle, ce qui n'est pas si mauvais tout compte fait.

Summary

Mathieu has just met Laura on Zack's birthday party and since then, he managed to have a date with her. When he picks her up from her place, she looks different from the one he met at the party: less makeup and a different personality. When they talk in the car, the engine starts making strange noises, after a while, it breaks down. What bad luck for a first date. But finally, although the date is ruined, Mathieu has the opportunity to talk with Laura and learn more about her, which is not so bad all things considered.

Vocabulaire / Vocabulary

travail - work

appartement - apartment

pâtés de maisons - blocks

trottoir - sidewalk

queue de cheval - ponytail

maquillage - make up

taches de rousseur - freckles

voiture - car

ceinture - seatbelt

radio - radio

GPS - GPS

cartographe - cartographer

rétroviseur - rearview mirror

virage - turn

moteur - engine

rugir - roaring on

roues - wheels

levier - leaver

capot - hood

sarcastiquement - sacarstically

paquet de cigarettes - pack of cigarettes

clin d'œil – wink of an eye

fumée - smoke

cendres - ashes

Questions

1 - Comment s'appellent les personnages de l'histoire ?

a. Les personnages s'appellent Mathieu et Laura.

b. Les personnages s'appellent Marc et Laura.

c. Les personnages s'appellent Mathieu et Clara.

2 - Quelle heure est-il quand Mathieu passe chercher Laura ?

a. Il est 11 heures.

b. Il est 10 heures.

b. Il est 15 heures.

3 - Quels vêtements portait Laura ?

a. Laura portait un jean et un capuchon.

b. Laura portait un jean et un t-shirt.

c. Laura portait une robe.

4 - Que fait Laura dans la vie ?

a. Laura est danseuse.

b. Laura est écrivain.

c. Laura est cartographe.

d. Laura est juriste.

5 - Que fait Mathieu dans la vie ?

a. Mathieu est étudiant en communication.

b. Mathieu est cartographe.

c. Mathieu est enseignant.

6 - Que se passe-t-il en chemin ?

7 - Que fait Mathieu quand il est stressé ?

8 - Que font Mathieu et Laura en attendant la dépanneuse ?

9 - Que penses Mathieu de Laura ?

10 - Pourquoi Mathieu ne croit-il pas au mariage ?

Questions

1-What are the names of the characters in the story?

a-The characters are called Mathieu and Laura

b-The characters are called Marc and Laura

c-The characters are called Mathieu and Clara

2-What time is it when Mathieu picks up Laura?

a-It is 11 am

b-It is 10 o'clock

b-It is 3 pm

3-What clothes is Laura wearing?

a-Laura was wearing jeans and a hoodie

b-Laura was wearing jeans and a t-shirt

c-Laura wore a dress

4-What does Laura do in life?

a-Laura is a dancer

b-Laura is a writer

c-Laura is a cartographer

d-Laura is a lawyer

5-What does Mathieu do in life?

a- Mathieu is studying communications

b- Mathieu is a cartographer

c- Mathieu is teaching

6-What's happening on the way?

7-What does Mathieu do when he is stressed?

8-What are Mathieu and Laura doing while waiting for the tow truck?

9-What does Mathieu think about Laura?

10-Why does Mathieu not believe in marriage?

Réponses

1 - a

2 - b

3 - b

4 - d

5 - a

6 - La voiture tombe en panne en chemin.

7 - Mathieu fume quand il est stressé.

8 - Mathieu et Laura parlent pendant qu'ils attendent la dépanneuse.

9 - Mathieu pense que Laura est douce, gentille et réfléchie. Elle pense beaucoup.

10 - Mathieu ne sait pas pourquoi. Il suppose que si c'est pour passer sa vie avec quelqu'un, il veut que ce soit avec quelqu'un qui en vaut la peine. Il n'a pas encore rencontré une telle personne.

Answers

1-a

2-b

3-b

4-d

5-a

5-Mathieu is in communications

6-The car breaks down on the way

7-Mathieu smokes when he is stressed

8-Mathieu and Laura talk as they wait for the wrecker.

9-Mathieu thinks Laura was sweet, kind and thoughtful. She thought a lot about things.

10-Mathieu does not know why. He assumes that if it's to spend his life with someone, he wants it to be with someone who is worth it. He has not met such a person yet.

Chapter 8 – Joyeuse fête

Je m'appelle Zoé et j'ai quarante-cinq ans. Depuis plusieurs mois, je rentre en retard du travail – trop de boulot ! Il fait nuit quand j'arrive enfin chez moi. Je monte les escaliers pour mon appartement et mes doigts froids cherchent clés. Henri m'a envoyé un message pour me dire qu'il sera lui aussi un peu en retard. Il devrait bientôt arriver. La porte s'ouvre et je cherche l'interrupteur en tâtonnant le mur.

Quand la lumière s'allume, je ne peux que voir la table du salon inondée de roses rouges. J'observe la scène. Les roses coûtent extrêmement chères. Qui pourrait se permettre ça ? Je ne connais personne qui gagne assez pour dépenser autant pour moi.

Il y a une note près des roses. Je la déplie et la lis.

Des excuses pour chaque rose.

D'un coup, je suis furieuse. Qui cela peut-être ? Comment est-ce qu'il ou elle sait où je vis ? Qui l'a laissé entrer chez moi ?

Je suis furieuse. Je prends mon téléphone et je compose le numéro de Marcello, le portier. Je me retourne et je quitte mon appartement en claquant la porte derrière moi. Je descends les marches jusqu'à l'entrée dans le hall.

« Marcello ! », crie-je, en marchant vers la réception. Il est le portier de l'immeuble depuis très longtemps et je lui fais confiance. Ou du moins, jusqu'à aujourd'hui. Je devrais peut-être y repenser.

« Qui êtes-vous pour laisser entrer des étrangers dans mon appartement ?

– Désolé, Madame Zoé, me dit-il.

« 'Désolé' ne va pas suffire. Et si c'était un tueur en série ?

– Avec des roses ? », s'interloque Marcello.

Je n'arrive pas à croire ce que j'entends.

« Vous ne pouvez pas laisser monter n'importe qui chez nous, surtout quand je ne suis pas à la maison. C'est réservé aux urgences. C'est dans mon contrat de location. »

Marcello hoche la tête.

« Je sais. Mais l'argent est plus fort qu'un contrat »

Je secoue la tête, encore plus énervée.

« On vous a soudoyé ? Où est votre dignité, monsieur, votre éthique professionnelle ?»

Marcello hausse les épaules.

« J'avais besoin d'argent. Ils m'ont donné une bien belle somme. »

De la fumée doit me sortir par les oreilles tant je suis furieuse.

« Vous ne pouvez pas juger les gens en fonction de combien ils sont prêts à vous donner.

– Mais vous pouvez le faire en fonction de la façon dont ils vous traitent. », déclare une voix derrière moi qui me fige sur placce.

Marcello regarde par-dessus mon épaule et sourit.

« Vous êtes de retour », dit Marcello.

Je me retourne lentement. Un jeune homme aux cheveux châtains, le teint pâle, et une jeune fille à la taille fine portant une robe fleurie, avec des boucles brunes et quelques taches de rousseurs sur son visage, se tiennent derrière moi et sourient. Mathieu et Marie !

« Que faites-vous ici ? je m'exclame, surprise.

– Quelle façon d'accueillir tes chères enfants, maman ! s'exclaffe le jeune homme.

– Joyeuse fête, maman, ajoute la jeune fille. Désolée de ne pas être venus pour les fêtes.

– Tu veux bien nous pardonner ? J'espère que tu ne nous fais pas la tête.

– Ou bien tu veux qu'on s'excuse de nouveau ?

– Vous l'avez déjà fait avec cette pluie de roses », je leur réponds en les prenant dans mes bras pour les embrasser.

Je prends une profonde inspiration, soulagée de la tournure des événements.

« Bon. Excuses acceptées. Vous venez en haut ? je demande. Nous n'avons pas beaucoup de place, mais nous avons du bon café. »

Ils sourient et hochent la tête. Je leur prends la main et nous montons les escaliers.

Je regarde par-dessus mon épaule vers Marcello.

« Ça ne veut pas dire que vous pouvez laisser des gens monter chez nous simplement parce qu'ils vous paient bien. Même s'ils ont des centaines de roses, dis-je. Juste pour cette fois… car ce sont mes enfants et qu'aujourd'hui, c'est la fête des mères ! »

My name is Zoe and I am 45. It's been a few months now that I come home late from work... I have way too much work. It's already dark when I get home. I climbed the stairs for my apartment and I look for the keys with my cold fingers. Henri sent me a message to tell me that he would also be late. He must be on his way home. The door swung open and I search for the light switch.

When the light turned on, I can only see my living room table, filled with red roses. I stared at the roses. I turned around and around.

Roses are expensive. Who could do something like this? I couldn't think of anyone that made enough money to spend this much on me.

There was a folded note on the table. I walked to it and picked up the note, unfolding it.

An apology for every rose.

I am suddenly furious. Who could it be? How the hell did they know where I lived? And who had let him or her in?

I turned around and left my apartment, slamming the door behind me.

I stormed down the stairs to the lobby.

"Marcello!" I shouted, walking to the front desk. He had been the doorman since I'd moved in here and I trusted him. Or at least, until today. I might have to rethink that.

"Who are you to let strangers enter my apartment?"

"I'm sorry, Madam Zoé," he said .

"Sorry isn't enough. What if it was a serial killer?"

"With roses?" Marcello asked.

I can't believe what I hear. "You can't just let anyone enter, especially when I'm not home. Only for emergencies. It's on my lease."

Marcello nodded. "I know. But money speaks louder than a lease..."

I shook my head, angrier than ever. "They bribed you? Where is your dignity, mister, your work ethic?"

Marcello shrugged. "I needed money. They gave me even more than I would have already accepted."

I shook my head. "You can't make hasty judgments on people based on how much they're willing to pay you."

"But you can do it based on how they treat you," a voice said behind me and I froze. Marcello looked over my shoulder and smiled.

"You are back." he said.

I turned around slowly. A young man with light brown hair, pale skin, and a light-haired girl wearing a flowery dress, with brown curls and a few freckles on her face were standing behind me, smiling. Mathieu and Marie!

 "What are you doing here?" I asked.

"Is that how you're supposed to welcome your dear kids?" said the young man.

"Happy Mother's Day," the girl added. "Sorry for not being there during the holidays."

"Could you forgive us? I hope you're not mad?"

"Or do you want us to apologize again?"

"You already did it with this thousand of roses," I smiled and hugged them.

I took a deep breath, relieved that everything turned out fine.

 "Okay," I said. "Apology accepted." I smiled. "Let's go upstairs?" I asked. "We don't have a lot of room but we have good coffee."

They smiled and nodded. I took their hands and we walked the stairs together.

I looked over my shoulder for Marcello.

"This doesn't mean that you can just let in anyone who bribes you. Even if they have thousands of roses," I said. "Just this time because they are my children. And because today, it's mother day."

Résumé

A 45 ans, Zoé vit avec son mari Henri dans un petit appartement. Un soir, lorsqu'elle rentre tard du travail, elle s'aperçoit que des gens se sont introduits chez elle. Sur sa table basse se trouvent plein de bouquets de roses. Son premier réflexe est d'aller voir Marcello, le portier, car il n'est pas sensé laisser des gens entrer sans permission. Alors qu'elle s'explique avec lui, les responsables arrivent derrière elle, et à sa grande surprise, ce sont ses enfants. Ils n'étaient pas venus la voir depuis longtemps. Elle avait d'ailleurs oublié qu'aujourd'hui c'était la fête des mères. A la fois surprise et heureuse, elle les invite à entrer chez elle.

Summary

Zoé is 45 and lives with her husband, Henri, in a small apartment. One evening when she comes back home late from work, she realizes that someone has entered her home. Her coffee table is full of roses. Her first instinct was to go talk to Marcello, the porter because he is not supposed to let people in without Zoe's permission. While she speaks with Marcello, the intruders arrive behind her and, to her surprise, it's her children. They did not visit for a long time. She had forgotten that today was Mother's Day. Both surprised and happy, she invites them inside the house.

Vocabulaire / Vocabulary

travail - work

escaliers - stairs

doigts - fingers

froid(s) - cold

clés - keys

interrupteur - light switch

salon - living room

cher - expensive

téléphone - phone

claquer - to slam

réception - front desk

avoir confiance - to trust

étrangers - strangers

tueur en série - serial killer

urgences - emergency

contrat de location - lease agreement

soudoyer - to bribe

éthique professionnelle – work ethic

épaules - shoulders

voix - voice

profond - deep

espace - space

café - coffee

fête des mères - Mother's day

Questions

1 - Quel âge a Zoé ?

a. 35 ans

b. 22 ans

c. 45 ans

2 - Que voit Zoé quand elle entre dans son appartement ?

a. Beaucoup de roses

b. Ses chats

c. Beaucoup de livres

3 - Quel est le nom du portier ?

a. Claudio

b. Antonio

c. Marcello

4 - Pourquoi Marcello a-t-il laissé entrer les gens dans l'appartement de Zoé ?

a. Parce qu'ils avaient l'air gentils

b. Parce qu'ils lui ont donné de l'argent en échange

c. Parce qu'il les connaissait

5 - Combien de fils et de filles Zoé a-t-elle ?

a. Deux fils et une fille

b. Deux filles et un fils

c. Un fils et une fille

6 - Pourquoi ses enfants sont-ils venus la voir tout d'un coup ?

7 - Pourquoi Zoé était-elle en colère contre Marcello ?

8 - Pourquoi Zoé ne s'attendait-elle pas à voir ses enfants ?

9 - Zoé est-elle contente de les voir ? Et pourquoi ?

10 - Va-t-elle les laisser entrer ?

1-How old is Zoé?

a-35

b-22

c-45

2-What does Zoé see when she enters her apartment?

a-A lot of roses

b-Her cats

c-A lot of books

3-What's the name of the doorman?

a-Claudio

b-Antonio

c-Marcello

4-Why did Marcello let the people enter in Zoé's apartment?

a-Because they looked nice

b-Because they gave him money in exchange

c-Because he knew them

5-How many sons and daughters does Zoé have?

a-Two sons and one daughter

b-Two daughters and one son

c-One son and one daughter

6-Why did her children came to visit her all of a sudden?

7-Why was Zoé mad at Marcello?

8-Why did Zoé did not expect to see her children?

9-Is Zoé happy seeing them? And why?

10-Did she let them in?

Réponses

1 - c

2 - a

3 - c

4 - b

5 - c

6 - Ils sont venus parce que c'est la fête des mères.

7 - Zoé était en colère contre Marcello parce qu'il laissait des étrangers entrer sans sa permission.

8 - Parce qu'elle ne les a pas vus depuis un moment.

9 - Zoé est heureuse parce qu'elle ne les a pas vus pendant les vacances.

10 - Elle les a invités pour un café.

Answers

1-c

2-a

3-c

4-b

5-c

6-They came because it was mother's day

7-Zoé was mad at Marcello because he let strangers in without her permission

8-Because she hasn't seen them for a while

9-Zoé is happy because she has not seen them for holidays.

10-She invited them over for a coffee.

Part 3: French Phrase Book

The Ultimate French Phrase Book for Traveling in France Including Over 1000 Phrases for Accommodations, Eating, Traveling, Shopping, and More

Introduction

If you're going to France for a couple of weeks or even just a few days, you should know some survival French - a few essential words and phrases that you'll use during your trip. There are plenty of language courses that will teach you how to deal with specific situations, like **asking for directions** or **going** somewhere. That being said, this book will not teach you French, it will just help you to find your way when you arrive to the airport or what you should say when you will go shopping, dining, or other daily activities.

This book is arranged according to theme and circumstances you will have to deal with as a tourist in France. Keep it with you. Whether you're a complete beginner or an advanced learner, this set of useful phrases will give you what you need.

So, let's get started.

Chapter 1 – Pronunciation

How to pronounce French the right way.

As you travel, you will always need to understand spoken French and will also need to make sure your interlocutor understands what you mean. That's the main purpose of this chapter. It is ok if you're a little bit nervous as long as they understand what you mean. It is not a big deal if you have a little accent.

The French alphabet

The French alphabet combines 26 letters. Standard French contains 13 oral vowels and up to 4 nasal vowels, but there are also **5 additional accented letters** that can be applied to change the sound of a letter.

a A [Ah]	n N [hun]
b B [Ba(y)]	o O [Oh]
c C [Sa(y)]	p P [Pay]
d D [Da(y)]	q Q [Coo]
e E [Uh]	r R [err]
f F [ayf]	s S [ess]
g G [zhay]	t T [tay]
h H [Ash]	u U[u]
i I [Eeh]	v V [vay]
j J[zhee]	w W[doub-leh-vey-]
k K [kah]	x X [eeks]
l L [ell]	y Y [ee-grek]
m M [hum]	z Z [zed]

Vowels:

A e i u o

Consonants:

B c d f g h j k l m m n p q r s t v w x y z

The French "R" is pronounced "Errr" as when you are about to spit. It is the best example to describe its sonority because only few languages use it. It sounds like a Spanish "J," or "La rota," as they say it.

The "Y" is pronounced as "ee" in English.

The Silent "h"

The "h" in French is a 100% silent letter no matter where it's located in a word. The only exception to this is when the preceding letter is "c," in which case the "ch" combination makes a "sh" sound or "k" sound.

"Housse" (Cover), for example, is pronounced "Ouss."

"Chaos" sounds like "Kaoh."

Single "s," Double "s" or "z"?

But it's just an "s," right? Pronouncing the "s" is more complicated than it seems.

The double "S" or "Ss" is pronounced like the end of the word "Bass".

The single "S" is pronounced like "Poison."

The single "S" and "Z" sound the same in French.

The difference between "é" "ait" et "et"

When you speak the following sentences, does the conjugation of the verb "parler" sound the same?

- J'ai parlé avec elle.
- Je parlais avec elle.

Many French learners will pronounce these in exactly the same way. In fact, they should not sound the same. This is surprising, but it's true.

"é" and "et" are pronounced "eh" while "Ait" or "ais" are pronounced like "May" without the "y" sound at the end.

How to Pronounce the French "u" Sound

There's no sound like the French "u" in English. It's not the same as an English "oo" sound. French has both the English "oo" and a distinct "u" sound, so you'll want to learn to pronounce them differently in order to avoid any misunderstandings.

For example, there aren't many scenarios where you can mix up the words "thanks a lot!" and "thanks, nice ass!" in French conversation and still be understood! So don't get your "merci beaucoup" and "merci beau cul" mixed up! To correctly pronounce the "u" sound, try this. Say a normal English "ee" sound (like at the end of the word "free"). Now, without moving your tongue, shape your lips into an "ooh" sound. Basically your lips are saying "oo" while your tongue is still saying "ee". And voilà! You have the French "u" sound!

Exercise: Try pronouncing the following pairs of words to really hear the difference between "u" and "ou":

- rue and roue

- en-dessus and en-dessous (these two have exact opposite meanings)

- cure and court

- juin and pingouin

Combination of vowels:

The combination of vowels in French gives a different sound that does not exist in the English language.

Ai [eh]

Ue [uay]

Oi [wah]

Oui [wee]

Ui [uee]

Combination of consonants with consonants

The combination of vowels with vowels is pronounced as in English (Cl, gu, qu etc ...) except for:

Ch [Shuh] but not Tch

Tr [Trrr] but not Tchr

Combination of vowels with consonants

We have seen the combinations of vowels with vowels; here we shall see the combinations of vowels with consonants. Why? Because their sound is different from English, they are combinations that are used over and over again in French.

Ail ille eil [ahy], [eey], [ayy]

On [On] (the "N" is silent, we do not pronounce it, we just keep the sound of the O in English)

Dropping the L in Your "il" and Your "elle"

Pronouncing your "il" and "elle" like French speakers is both easier than pronouncing it the "proper" way, and an effective way to make your colloquial speech sound much more natural.

Consider the following two sounds:

ee-lee-ya

ee-ya

Say each sound aloud several times in a row. Which one can you say more quickly and easily? When it comes to the phrase "il y a", French speakers simplify it to sound like "ee-ya". A couple of examples:

- Est-ce qu'il y a quelqu'un? (Is there someone out there ?)

- Oui, il y a quelqu'un (Yes, there is.)

It doesn't end there, however. In everyday French conversation, particularly when you're speaking quickly, you can drop the L from "il" and "elle" in the majority of sentences! This is especially true when the next word in the sentence starts with a consonant. Here are some examples:

- Qu'est-ce qu'il boit? ("skee" boit)

- Elle connait mon frère ("eh" connait)

- Il veut ça ("ee" veut)

- Je veux qu'elle réponde à mes questions ("keh" réponde)

The Real Way to Pronounce "d" and "t" Before the Letter "i"

Here's a little tip you can use in your pronunciation that will make you sound closer to the native pronunciation. Think of the French word "appétit". How should you pronounce the second syllable? Lots of French learners would answer that you pronounce it like the English word "tea", but this isn't entirely true if you listen carefully. It sounds more like "Peutzi."

Next time you're listening to a native French speaker, listen for this sound in these types of syllables and make an effort to imitate them. Even though it's a subtle sound, it's noticeable enough that French speakers themselves wouldn't notice it immediately.

Exercise: Here are some words to practice with:

routine

petit

gentil

dieu

"En"/"an" and "in"

These are the characteristically "nasal" sounds that are a dead giveaway to non-French speakers which are really not difficult for anglophones to master. It doesn't help that the "in"/"ain" sound in France sounds more like the "en"/an" sound in Quebec!

For "en"/"an", try saying the word "song", but stop just before your throat closes into the "ng" sound. You've just pronounced the French word cent (or sang, s'en, sans).

For "in"/"ain"/"eint", say the word "clang" but stop just before your throat closes into the "ng" sound. You've just pronounced the French word "pain"(bread). Easy!

The matter can be a bit more difficult for French learners, if they overthink it and end up pronouncing it like "en"/"an". Here are a few examples to let you hear the difference:

emporter and importer

grattant and gratin

étant and éteint

lentement and lendemain

The Final Consonant

There are many French letters that simply aren't pronounced at the end of words. In general, the final consonants of a word are usually silent in French except in some cases of the letters c, f, l or r.

Let's take a look at some examples of silent consonants at the end of words:

froid (Frwaa)

cold

grand (Grhun)

big/large

Beaucoup (Bokoo)

a lot/many/much

Petit (Puhtee)

Little

How to pronounce French vowels

Vowels in French can have accent marks; except for "e", this doesn't usually change the sound:

a, à, â	like "a" in "father"
e	like "a" in "about"
é	like "ay" in "say"

ê	like "e" in "set"
è	like "e" in "set"
i, î	like "ee" in "feed"
o, o, ô, au, eau	like "oa" in "boat" or "aw" in "law"
ou	like "oo" in "food", but a pure vowel
u, ù	more or less like "oo" in "food", but the tongue is like "ee" in "feed"; written uu in transcriptions
y	like "ee" in "feed"

How to pronounce French consonants

There are many French consonants that are usually dropped: parlez (speak) is pronounced parhl-AY, not parhl-AYZ; tort (wrong) is pronounce tor, not tort. Also a final "e" is usually silent. But if the next word begins with a vowel, the consonant may be pronounced; this is called liaison.

We're going to see how to pronounce French diphthongs or gliding vowels

a	like "i" in "fight", like "ay" in "hay" (at the end of a word)
ail	like "i" in "fight"
ais	like "ea" in "bread" (at the end of a word)
au, eau	like "ow" in "blow"
an	nasal; kind of like "ahng", but without the hard "g" at the end
eu	between "ew" in "dew" and "ur" in "burp"; written eu in transcriptions
œ	more or less like "eu", slightly more "open"
er	like "ay" in "hay" -- usually found at the end of word/verb
ez	like "ay" in "hay"
en, em	nasal; same as "an"

in	nasal; like "ang" in "Tang", but without the hard "g" at the end
oi	like "wa" in "walk"
oin	nasal; like "wang", but without the hard "g" at the end
ou	like "oo" in "food"
on	nasal; like "ong" in "long", but without the hard "g" at the end
oui	like "wee" in "week"
ui	like "wee" in "week", but with the tongue forward
un	nasal; like "ung" in "hung", but without the hard "g" at the end
ch	like "sh" in "bush"
gn	like "ny" in "canyon". This is particularly difficult when followed by oi, as in baignoire (beh-NYWAR) "bathtub".t
il	like "y" in "three years", with some exceptions (ville is veel)
ll	like "l"
ph	like "f" in "fun"
tch	like "ch" in "chew" (but kind of rare)
th	like "t" in "tin"
tr	"t" followed by a short gargle

Chapter 2 – Essentials and basics

There are some phrases that are particularly helpful to international travelers. Below are several phrases that might come in handy during your stay in a French-speaking country.

Greetings

Bonjour/ Hello

Bonjour (après-midi)/ Good afternoon

Salut/ Hello/ Hi

Bonsoir/ Good evening

Bonne nuit/ Good night

French Phrases for Meeting and Greeting

Parlez-vous anglais ?/ Do you speak English?

Est-ce qu'il y a quelqu'un qui parle anglais ?/ Does anyone here speak English?

Excusez mon français./ Excuse my poor French.

Je ne parle qu'un petit peu de français./ I only speak a little French.

Comment vous appelez-vous ?/ What is your name?

Je m'appelle Florence./ My name is Florence.

Voici Florence./ This is Florence.

Comment allez-vous ?/ How are you?

Est-ce que tout va bien ?/ How have you been?

Je vais bien, merci./ I'm fine, thank you.

Je suis très heureux de vous rencontrer./ I am very glad to meet you.

J'ai été très heureux de faire votre connaissance./ It was nice meeting you.

Je ne comprends pas./ I don't understand.

Qu'avez-vous dit ?/ What did you say?

Pouvez-vous parler plus lentement ?/ Could you speak more slowly?

Je comprends parfaitement./ I understand perfectly.

Leaving

Au revoir/ Goodbye

A plus tard/ See you later

French Phrases for leaving

Je dois y aller./ I've got to leave.

Je dois partir./ I've got to go.

A plus/ See you.

A la prochaine/ See you next time

Au revoir/ Goodbye

Adieu/ Farewell

Bon voyage/ Good trip

On se revoit bientôt./ See you soon.

J'aimerais rester plus longtemps mais je dois aller quelque part./ I'd like to stay a little bit longer but I've got to go somewhere.

Je dois vous laisser./ I need to go.

Saying thank you

Merci/ Thanks

Merci beaucoup !/ Thanks a lot.

Merci pour votre aide./ Thank you for your help.

Merci (beaucoup)/ Thank you (very much).

Je vous en prie./ Don't mention it.

Non merci./ No, thank you.

Being polite

S'il vous plaît/ Excuse me!/Please

Je vous en prie/ You're welcome

Pardon/ Excuse me

Excusez-moi/ Excuse me

Je m'excuse./ I apologize

Je suis désolé(e)/ I'm sorry

Il n'y a pas de quoi/ You're welcome/Don't mention it (In response to people who thank you).

Other

D'accord/ OK

Pardon !/ Sorry

Où sont les toilettes s'il vous plaît ?/ Excuse me, where are the toilets?

Wishes:

Bonne année !/ Happy New Year!

Bon anniversaire !/ Happy birthday!

Joyeuses fêtes !/ Happy holiday!

Félicitations !/ Congratulations!

Joyeux Noël/ Merry Christmas

Forbidden

Interdit/ Forbidden

Attention/ Caution

Danger/ Danger

Questions

Je voudrais .../ I'd like ...

Où est ... ?/ Où sont ... ?/ Where is ... ? /Where are ... ?

Ah bon ? C'est vrai ?/ Really?

Comment ?/ How?

Pourquoi ?/ Why?

Quoi ?/ What?

Où ?/ Where?

Quand ?/ When?

Asking your way

Pouvez-vous me montrer où ça se trouve ?/ Can you show me where that is?

Est-ce que je peux vous demander mon chemin ?/ May I ask you for directions?

Basic French dialog

Bonjour./ Good morning.
Est-ce que vous parlez anglais ?/ Do you speak English?

Je suis désolé./ I'm sorry.
Je ne parle pas anglais./ I do not speak English.

Malheureusement je ne parle qu'un petit peu de français./ Unfortunately, I only speak a little French.

Ça ne fait rien./ That's all right.
Je vous comprends./ I understand you.

Ça me rend nerveux de parler français./ I get nervous when I speak French.

Je vous comprends très bien./ I understand you very well.

Common expressions in French:

What a rip off!/ Ça coûte les yeux de la tête!

Keep the change!/ Gardez la monnaie !

Pull the other one!/ A d'autres !

Bless you!/ A tes souhaits !

By the way/ Au fait

Chat someone up/ Bavarder avec quelqu'un

Bon apetit./ Bon appétit !

It rings a bell./ Ça me rappelle quelque chose

It serves you right./ Ça t'apprendra !

Keep your hair on!/ Calme-toi !

By all means/ Certainement

It's up to you./ C'est à toi de voir.

How come?/ Comment ça se fait ?

Cheer up!/ Courage !

Cross your fingers!/ Croise les doigts !

To my mind/ D'après moi

You're welcome/ De rien

Hurry up!/ Dépêche-toi !

Say when/ Dis-moi quand

Let's have one for the road!/ Et un pour la route !

Watch out!/ Fais attention !

Make yourself at home./ Fais comme chez toi!

Were you born in a field/barn?/ Ferme la porte !

I must be off./ Je dois y aller.

I haven't got a clue./ Je n'en ai aucune idée.

Leave me alone!/ Laisse-moi tranquille !

A quid/ Une livre sterling

Better late than never./ Mieux vaut tard que jamais.

Same here/ Pareil

No wonder/ Pas étonnant !

To pay cash/ Payer cash

Talk of the devil/ Quand on parle du loup !

What a cheek!/ Quel culot !

What a mess!/ Quel désordre !

Cheers!/ Santé !

Get the sack/ Se faire mettre à la porte

Really!/ Sérieux ?

Help yourself/ Sers-toi

If only/ Si seulement

Pissed as a newt/ Rond comme une barrique

Touch wood/ Touche du bois

You're pulling my leg./ Tu me fais marcher.

You're kidding./ Tu plaisantes.

A pain in the arse/ Un emmerdeur

A wet blanket/ Un rabat-joie

A hangover/ Une gueule de bois

Let the cat out of the bag/ Vendre la mèche

Times of the day

lever du soleil	sunrise
aube	dawn
matin, matinée	morning
midi	noon
après-midi	afternoon
soirée, soir [Am]	evening
crépuscule	dusk
nuit	night
minuit	midnight

Asking for the time:

Expressions:

Quelle heure est-il ?

Est-ce que vous avez l'heure, s'il vous plaît ?

English	French
When did you get here?	Quand est-ce que tu es arrivé ici ?
Today	Aujourd'hui
Yesterday	Hier
October	Octobre
November	Novembre
December	Décembre
What time are you leaving at?	Tu pars à quelle heure ?
Morning, at eight o'clock	Le matin, à huit heures
Morning, at a quarter past 8	Le matin, à huit heures quinze
Morning, at half past 8	Le matin, à huit heures trente
Morning, at a quarter to nine	Le matin, à huit heures quarante cinq
Evening, at 6pm	Le soir, à dix-huit heures
I am late	Je suis en retard

The days of the week

Lundi	Monday
Mardi	Tuesday
Mercredi	Wednesday
Jeudi	Thursday
Vendredi	Friday

Samedi   Saturday

Dimanche Sunday

Expressions:

Quel jour est-il ? What day is it?

Or Quel jour sommes-nous ?

Nous sommes dimanche.

Or just

C'est dimanche.

 The date

The date is really simple in French.

It is pronounced just after the day (lundi, mardi, vendredi etc.) and "Le" is put before the day.

Ex: Quel jour sommes-nous ? What day is it?

Nous sommes le mardi 15 août 2017. We are on Tuesday 15 August 2017.

We use the ordinal number "1er" or "Premier" only for the first day of the month .

Other useful expressions :

day	jour; journée
week	semaine
a fortnight	quinzaine
month	mois
monthly	mensuel
quarter	quart, trimester
year	an, année
a leap-year	année bissextile
century	siècle
the day before yesterday	avant-hier

yesterday	hier
today	aujourd'hui, de nos jours
tomorrow	demain
the day after tomorrow	après-demain

Denominations of francs and euros:

The euro, like the franc, is counted in centimes, like our cents. Coins and bills are minted for:

1 centime

5 centimes

10 centimes

20 centimes

50 centimes

1 euro

2 euros

5 euros

10 euros

20 euros

50 euros

100 euros

200 euros

500 euros

Chapter 3 – Transport

Once you land in France, the first place where you're going to be is in the airport.

So here we go.

The airport

Whether you are planning to travel to a French-speaking destination or not, in this chapter we will share with you a list of vocabulary and phrases related to airports. Many large cities across have an international airport: Paris, of course, but also Bordeaux, Lyon, Marseille, Nice, Strasbourg, and Toulouse . It helps if you correctly know how to pronounce the names of the airports in France, such as the Paris-Charles-de-Gaulle, and a few French airport vocabulary words.

When asking your way, you don't need to introduce yourself. A simple "Bonjour, pouvez-vous m'aider ?" (Hello, can you help me?) is okay. What will follow depends on the answer you will get if it is a "Bien sûr" (Of course) or a "Désolé. Non." (Sorry).

If the answer is "Oui", here are the common phrases you're going to use. Can you imagine how confusing it could be when you're in a foreign airport where people are communicating only in French?

Greetings

Bonjour/ Hello

Bonjour Monsieur/ Hello Sir

Bonjour Madame/Mademoiselle/ Hello Mrs/Miss

Asking for language

Parlez-vous anglais ?/ Do you speak English?

⇒ Oui, je parle anglais./⇒ Yes, I speak English.

⇒ Non, désolé./⇒ No, I don't. Sorry.

Je parle (un peu) français./ I speak (a little) French.

Introduce yourself

Of course we have seen above that you don't really need to introduce yourself when asking your way. But sometimes it is necessary, especially if you feel you are still a beginner and can't handle a proper talk with a native speaker. Just in case you feel your interlocutor will not understand what you mean and you want to prepare them to listen carefully and to be patient, here are the basic phrases you need to know.

Bonjour, je viens de _____./ Hello, I am from _____.

Parlez-vous anglais ?/ Do you speak English?

Je parle (un peu) français./ I speak (a little) French.

Parlez-vous français ?/ Do you speak French?

⇒ Oui, je parle français./⇒ Yes, I speak French.

Or

⇒ Non, désolé./⇒ No, I don't. Sorry.

If you don't understand what they say or if they speak too fast

Comment ? Pardon ?/ What?

Je ne comprends pas./ I don't understand.

Je ne comprends pas ce que vous dites./ I don't understand what you said.

Je ne parle pas bien français./ I don't speak French very well.

Pouvez-vous traduire pour moi ?/ Can you translate for me?

Then ask them politely to repeat it

Qu'est-ce que vous avez dit ?/ What did you say?

Répétez, s'il vous plaît./ Repeat, please.

Pouvez-vous répéter s'il vous plaît ?/ Can you repeat, please?

If you still don't understand because they speak too fast and don't articulate enough

Plus lentement/ More slowly

Plus lentement s'il vous plaît/ More slowly, please

Est-ce que vous pouvez parler plus lentement, s'il vous plaît ?/ Could you speak more slowly, please?

Encore une fois/ One more time

Dites-le encore, s'il vous plaît./ Please say that again.

Asking general questions/ Introducing a question

J'ai un problème./ I have a problem.

J'ai une question./ I have a question.

Je suis perdu./ I'm lost.

J'ai besoin de renseignements./ I need some information.

Que veut dire ___ ?/ What does ___ mean?
Comment dit-on ___ en français ?/ How do you say ___ in French?
Comment dit-on en anglais ?/ What is this in English?
Comment ça se dit en anglais ?/ How do you say that in English?

Comment on écrit ça ?/ How do you spell it?

Asking for direction

Pouvez-vous me montrer où ça se trouve ?/ Can you show me where that is?

Est-ce que je peux vous demander mon chemin ?/ May I ask you for directions?

Searching something or losing something

Je ne trouve pas mes bagages./ I can't find my luggage.

Je ne trouve pas mon bagage à main./ I can't find my hand luggage.

Je ne trouve pas ma valise./ I can't find my suitcase.

J'ai perdu quelque chose./ I lost something.

Il y a quelque chose que je ne trouve pas./ There's something I can't find.

Où est mon (Name of the thing you can't find) ?/ Where is my (Name of the thing you can't find)?

Searching a place to go or to sleep

Où est l'hôtel ?/ Where is the hotel?

Où est-ce que je peux trouver un hôtel ?/ Where can I find a hotel?

Où se trouve l'hôtel le plus proche ?/ Where is the closest hotel?

Il y a des hôtels dans le coin ?/ Are there hotels in the neighborhood?

Où allez-vous ?/ Where are you going?

If there are people you know that will come and pick you up at the airport then this is what you should say to strangers:

C'est bon, j'attends quelqu'un./ It is ok, I am waiting for someone.

Je cherche quelqu'un./ I am looking for someone.

J'attends quelqu'un./ I am waiting for someone.

Il y a déjà quelqu'un vient me chercher./ Someone's already picking me up.

If not, then you should find a taxi.

Waiting for a taxi

In order to determine if a taxi is available or not, just watch the illuminated white box situated on its roof: if it is lit red, then it's occupied; if it is lit green, then it's available. There's a unique number to call (01 45 30 30 30) in place and it allows you to call taxis equipped with a terminal. Through an automated assistant, you can choose which arrondisement and station is the nearest to you. If the station then doesn't respond, you will be automatically connected to a second or third in proximity.

French Phrases to hail a taxi

Où puis-je prendre un taxi ?/ Where can I get a taxi?

Taxi !/ Taxi!

Taxi: Où allez-vous ?/ Where would you like to go?

You: Je vais à la (mention the place you want to go)./ I'm going to the (The name of the place).

Pourriez-vous m'emmener à cet hôtel ?/ Can you take me to this hotel, please?

Je vais à l'hôtel (Say the name of the hotel)./ I'm going to the (Name of the hotel).

Amenez-moi ici s'il vous plaît./ Take me there, please.

Pouvez-vous prendre mes bagages ?/ Can you take my luggage?

Je vais à cette adresse./ I'm going to this address.

Je vais à cet endroit./ I'm going to this place.

Distance

Est-ce loin d'ici ?/ Is it far from here?

Non, c'est à côté./ No, it is close.

Oui, c'est un peu plus loin./ Yes it's a little bit further away.

Prenez votre temps./ Take your time.

C'est à droite./ You go right.

C'est à gauche./ You go left.

C'est tout droit./ It's straight on.

C'est ici./ It's right here.

C'est par là./ It's that way.

Stop./ Stop.

Arrêtez-vous là./Stop.

Pay the taxi

Combien cela va coûter ?/ How much will it be?

Ça fera combien ? Ça fait combien ?/ How much will it be?

Je vous doit combien ?/ How much should I pay?

Pouvez-vous me donner un ticket s'il vous plaît ?/ Can I have a receipt, please?

Thanks

Merci/ Thanks

Merci beaucoup/ Thanks a lot

Bonne soirée/ Good evening

Bonne journée/ Have a nice day

Vocabulary:

Carte d'embarquement/ Boarding pass

Bagages/ Luggage

Valise/ Suitcase

Sécurité/Douane/ Security/Customs

Enregistrement/ Check-in

Porte/ Gate

Agent de bord/ Flight attendant

Billet d'avion/ Plane ticket

Billet simple/ One-way ticket

Billet aller-retour/ Round-trip ticket

Passeport/ Passport

Visa/ Visa

A few common questions that could be helpful during your trip.

Quand est-ce que je dois être à la porte ?	When do I have to be at the gate?
Vous devez vous présenter à la porte 30 minutes avant l'heure du départ.	You have to be at the gate 30 minutes prior to departure.
Combien de temps dure le vol ?	How long is the flight?
Combien de temps va-t-on s'arrêter ?	How long is the stopover?
Est-ce que j'ai besoin d'un visa ?	Do I need a visa?
Vous n'avez pas besoin de visa.	You won't need a visa.
Combien de valises est-ce que je peux prendre ?	How many pieces of luggage can I take?
Vous pouvez prendre seulement un bagage à main.	You can only take one piece of hand luggage.
Je voudrais avoir un siège du côté hublot, s'il vous plaît.	I would like to have a window seat, please.
Malheureusement, nous n'avons plus de siège disponible du côté hublot.	Unfortunately, we don't have any window seats left.
Je voudrais avoir un siège du côté couloir s'il vous plaît.	I would like to have an aisle seat, please.

The train station

There are 5 main train stations in Paris: Gare du Nord, Gare de l'Est, Gare de Lyon, Gare d'Austerlitz and Gare Montparnasse.

Finding the station

Où est la gare / station de bus / centre-ville ?/ Where is the station / next bus-station / city center?

Bonjour, où est la gare / station de bus / centre-ville ?/ Hello, where is the railway station / next bus-station / city center?

Bonjour, je cherche la gare./ Hello I'm looking for the station.

Bonjour, je suis perdu, où est la gare ?/ Hello, I'm lost, where is the station?

Bonjour, pouvez-vous l'aider à trouver la gare ?/ Hello, could you help me to find the station?

Salut, je suis étranger, où est la gare s'il-vous-plaît ?/ Hi, I'm a foreigner, may I know where the station is?

Distance

A quelle distance est le centre-ville / la station de bus la plus proche ?/ How far is it to the city center / to the next bus station?

⇒Pas loin d'ici./ ⇒Not far from here. (Possible reply)

C'est à quelle distance ?/ How far is it?

NOTE: Once they reply, don't forget to say "Merci" (Thank you) because if you leave without saying "Merci", it's rude.

Buying tickets

Always start with a « Bonjour »

Où va ce train s'il vous plaît ?/ Where does this train go, please?

Où puis-je acheter un billet ?/ Where can I buy a ticket?

Un billet pour (Place) s'il-vous-plaît./ A ticket for (Place), please.

Quel est le prix du billet pour (Name of the place) s'il vous plaît ?/ How much is a ticket to (Place)?

Je voudrais un aller simple (un aller-retour) pour Paris s'il-vous-plaît./ A single (return) to Paris please.

Je voudrais un billet pour Paris s'il-vous-plaît./ A ticket to Paris please.

Waiting for the train

Avez-vous les horaires des trains ?/ Do you have the train's time table?

Quand arrive le train pour (Name of the place you want to go) ?/ When will the train for (Place) will arrive?

Le train est en retard./ The train is delayed.

Est-ce-que ce train s'arrête à (Place) ?/ Does this train stop at (Place)?

Quand est-ce que part le train pour (Place) ?/ When does the train for (Place) leave?

Toilet

Où puis-je trouver des toilettes ?/ Where can I find a toilet?

Y a-t-il des toilettes près d'ici ?/ Is there a toilet near here?

J'aimerais aller aux toilettes./ I would like to go to the toilet.

Où sont les toilettes ?/ Where is the restroom?

Missing the train

Bonjour, j'ai raté mon train./ Hello, I missed my train.

A quelle heure part le prochain train pour Paris ?/ When does the next train for Paris leave?

Savez-vous quand le prochain train arrive ?/ Do you know when will the next train arrive?

Vocabulary:

gare/ train station

quai/ platform

hall de gare/ station hall

salle d'attente/ waiting room

le guichet/ the ticket office

un billet/ a ticket

tarif (de train)/ (train) fare

carte d'abonnement/ season ticket

horaire, tableau des horaires/ timetable

un aller-retour/ a return ticket

un aller-simple/ a single ticket

la consigne automatique/ left luggage locker

le chef de gare/ the station master

bureau des renseignements, accueil/ information desk

contrôleur/ ticket inspector

conducteur de train/ train driver

un chariot à bagages/ a (luggage) trolley

monter dans le train/ to get on the train

descendre du train/ to get off the train

voie ferrée/ track

train express/ express train

train rapide/ fast train

voyage en train/ train trip

The bus station

Travelling in France is easy. There are many ways to move, such as subways and airports, but the cheapest one is the public transport.

Several cities offer a rather expansive bus network.

Paris et Ile-de-France: Transilien SNCF

Lille: Transpole

Strasbourg: Compagnie des transports Strabourgeois

Nantes: Transports en commun de l'agglomération Nantaise

Rennes: Service de transport en commun de Rennes

Lyon: Transports en commun Lyonnais

Marseille: Régie des transports de Marseille

Bordeaux: Tram et bus de la communauté urbaine de Bordeaux

Toulouse: Transports en commun de l'agglomération Toulousaine

S'il vous plaît ! Je cherche l'arrêt de bus. / Excuse me! I'm looking for the bus stop.

Est-ce qu'il y a un arrêt de bus près d'ici ?/ Is there a bus stop near here?

Quand part le bus ?/ When does the bus leave?

L'autobus est à l'heure./ The bus is on time.

Possible reply if you missed it:

⇒Votre bus est parti il y a une heure./ Your bus left an hour ago.

⇒Vous avez raté votre bus./ You missed your bus.

⇒Vous l'avez raté./ You missed it.

So you can say:

A quelle heure part le prochain bus pour (Place) ?/ When does the next train for (Place) leave?

Fuel

Bonjour, faites-moi le plein s'il vous plaît./ A full tank, please.

Les horaires des bus/ Bus schedule

Le garage de réparation/ The garage

La station d'essence/ The petrol station

Essence, s'il-vous-plaît./ Fuel, please.

The Subway

During your journey, you will find that a subway is a great way to get from one place to another. And most French people take it daily. The subway is almost like the train, so you just have to repeat the same text as you did in the train sation.

Schedule, opening time, metro

The Paris metro closes around 1:00 am and around 2:00 am on the weekend. The metro starts again in the morning a bit before 6 am.

There are free maps at the ticket windows. Once you have your ticket, keep it until you leave the station. RATP staff members often check tickets and you might be fired if you can't prove you have a valid ticket. A tone will sound when the doors to the train are about to close. You only have 2-3 seconds and the doors will close on you (whether you're fully in the train or not). In order to familiarize you with the subway, here are the basic vocabularies related to the subway.

Transport vocabulary

Métro/ Subway

Sation de métro/ Subway station

Une automobile/ Car

Une moto/ Motorbike

Un camion/ Truck/Lorry

Un autobus/ Bus

Un car/ Coach

Un camionette/ Van

Une remorque/ Trailer

Une caravane/ Caravan

Une motocyclette/ Moped

Une bicyclette/ Bicycle

Un avion/ Aircraft

Un bateau/ Boat, ship

Une péniche/ Barge

Une aéroglisseur/ Hovercraft

Un train/ Train

Boat trip:

anchorage	mouillage
berth	couchette
boarding	embarquement
bridge	passerelle, poste de pilotage
cabin, stateroom	cabine
cabin with balcony	cabine balcon
chief engineer	le chef machine
chief purser	le commissaire principal
chief radio	le chef radio
courtesy flag	pavillon de courtoisie

crew, staff	équipage
cruise	croisière
deck	pont
dinghy	canot
disturbance	perturbation
dock, pier	quai
docked	posté à quai
draft	tirant d'eau
flag	pavillon
foredeck	avant-pont
gangway	passerelle
gross registered tonnage	jauge brute
harbour, port	port
head officers	état-major
high water	pleine mer
horn	corne
jetty, pier	jetée
knot speed	vitesse exprimée en noeuds
life boat drill	exercice de sécurité
life buoy	bouée de sauvetage
life-jacket	gilet de sauvetage
lighthouse	phare
liner	paquebot
log (book)	journal de bord
muster station	point de rassemblement

	no view cabin	cabine intérieure
	outside view cabin	cabine vue extérieure
	passageway	coursive
to	pitch	tanguer
	port of call	escale
	port side	bâbord
	porthole	hublot
	propeller	hélice
	prow, bow	proue
	reception desk, information desk	bureau d'information
	rescue boat	bateau de sauvetage
	rolling	roulis
to	sail [leave the harbour]	appareiller
to be	seasick	avoir le mal de mer
	seating	service de restauration
	staff captain	le commandant en second
	starboard (side)	tribord
	stern, aft	poupe
	storm warning	avis de tempête
	swell	houle
	time zone	fuseau horaire
	tonnage	tonnage
	total passenger capacity	capacité totale passagers
	weather forecast	prévisions météorologiques

Finance & Business

Business French

an account	un compte
an accountant	un comptable
an acquisition	un rachat d'entreprise
an advantage	un avantage
to advertise	faire la publicité
an advertisement	une annonce publicitaire
an advertising campaign	une campagne publicitaire
to afford	avoir les moyens d'acheter, pouvoir payer
the after-sales service	le service après-vente
an agenda	un ordre du jour
an appointment	une nomination
to approve	approuver, ratifier
the Articles of Association	les statuts
an assembly line	une chaîne de montage
to audit the accounts	vérifier les comptes, auditer les comptes
an auditor	un commissaire aux comptes
the balance	le solde
a balance sheet	un bilan
a bank	une banque
the assets (in a balance)	l'actif
the liabilities	le passif
a bankruptcy	une faillite

a	bargain	une affaire
to	be in the red (accounting)	être déficitaire
to	be in the black (accounting)	être positif
	benchmarking	un étalonnage, une référenciation
a	bill (accounting)	une note, une facture (à payer)
	the board of directors	le conseil d'administration
	bookkeeping	la comptabilité
a	book-keeper	un comptable
to	borrow	emprunter
a	branch	une agence, une succursale
a	brand	une marque
	the branding	marquage, branding
to	break a contract	violer un contrat, rompre un contrat
a	budget	un budget
	the business	le commerce, les affaires
	business is brisk	les affaires tournent
	business is slack	les affaires sont calmes
	business connections	les relations d'affaires
a	business contract	un contrat commercial
	business hours	heures ouvrables
	business intelligence	veille économique
a	business plan	un plan d'affaires
to	buy	acheter
to	buy in bulk	acheter en gros
a	buyer	un acheteur

to	cancel an order	annuler une commande
an	channel of distribution	un canal de distribution
to	charge for (payment)	faire payer
	cheap	bon marché
	co-branding	le cogriffage, alliance de marques
to	come to maturity	arriver à échéance
a	Chartered Accountant (CA)	un expert-comptable
	COD (cash on delivery)	paiement comptant à la livraison
a	commercial traveller	un représentant
a	commercial network	un réseau commercial
a	commission	une commission, une commande
to	launch a product	lancer un produit
a	company	une société
the	competition	la compétition
	competitive intelligence	veille à la concurrence
a	competitor	un concurrent
to	compete with	concourir, rivaliser avec, être en concurrence avec
to	complain	se plaindre
to	conduct à survey	mener une enquête
to	confirm	confirmer, corroborer
to	consider	considérer, examiner, songer
to	consign	expédier, envoyer
a	consignment note	un bordereau d'expédition
a	consultant	un conseiller
a	consumer	un consommateur

	consumerism	la défense du consommateur
to	convince	convaincre
a	corporation	une société
	costs	coûts
to	cost	coûter
a	creditor	un créancier
a	customer	un client
	customs duties	droits de douane
	CWO (cash with order)	paiement comptant à la commande
a	deadline	date limite
the	debt	la dette
a	debtor	débiteur
to	decide	décider
to	decrease	réduire, diminuer
to	deliver	distribuer, livrer
	delivery	distribution, livraison
the	domestic trade	le commerce intérieur
the	external trade	le commerce extérieur
the	foreign trade	le commerce extérieur
	debt collection	recouvrement de créance
a	demand	une demande
a	department	rayon, département, service
	deregulation	déréglementation
to	develop	développer
	direct mailing	publipostage direct

	direct marketing	vente directe
a	disadvantage	un inconvénient, un désavantage
a	discount	une réduction
to	dispatch	envoyer
to	distribute	distribuer
to	employ	employer
an	employee	un employé, une employée
	empowerment	renforcement d'équipe
an	equipment	un équipement, un équipage
to	establish	fonder, créer, établir
to	establish a business	créer une entreprise
to	estimate	estimer
to	exchange	échanger
the	expenses	les frais, les dépenses
	expensive	coûteux
	overhead expenses	les frais généraux
to	extend	étendre
the	facilities	équipement
	retail facilities	équipement commercial
a	feedback	un retour d'information, un feedback
to	file for bankruptcy	déposer le bilan
to	find a niche	trouver un créneau
a	firm	une entreprise, une firme
to	found a business	créer une entreprise
to	fund	financer

to	get better	s'améliorer
to	get worse	s'empirer
to	go bankrupt	faire faillite
the	goods	la marchandise, les articles
the	growth	la croissance
a	guarantee	une garantie
to	honour a contract	exécuter un contrat, réaliser un contrat
a	hoarding [GB] (= billboard)	un panneau publicitaire
a	billboard [US] (=hoarding)	un panneau publicitaire
the	head office	le siège social
to	improve	améliorer
the	income tax	l'impôt sur le revenu
to	increase	augmenter
the	industry	l'industrie
an	interest (finance)	intérêt
an	inventory	un inventaire
to	invest	investir
an	invoice	une facture (à faire payer)
to	invoice	facturer
to	join a trade union	se syndiquer
the	lay-off	le chômage temporaire
to	lend	prêter
	life cycle	cycle de vie
a	limited liability company	une société à responsabilité limitée
a	loss	une perte

to	lower	baisser
	loyalty	la fidélité
to	maintain	maintenir, entretenir
to	make money	faire de l'argent, faire des bénéfices
to	manage	gérer, diriger
the	management	la direction
the	margin	la marge
the	market	le marché
the	market leader	le leader sur le marché
a	market survey	une étude de marché
a	market share	une part de marché
to	measure	mesurer
	merchandise	les marchandises
to	merchandise	commercialiser
a	merger	une fusion d'entreprise
a	niche	un créneau
to	obtain	obtenir
an	offer	une offre
an	order	un ordre
to	order	commander, ordonner
to	organize	organiser
an	outlet	un point de vente
to	owe (I owe him 100 euros)	devoir (Je lui dois 100 euros)
to	own	posséder, être propriétaire
	packaging	l'emballage, le conditionnement

to	pay	payer
to	pay by instalments	payer en plusieurs versements
a	payment	un paiement
	penalty	peine, condamnation
to	plan	planifier
a	preliminary contract	un avant-contrat
the	price	le prix
to	process	traiter, opérer, procéder
to	produce	produire
a	product	un produit
	production	la production
	profit	le bénéfice
	profit margin	la marge bénéficiaire
the	profitability	la rentabilité
to	promote	promouvoir
a	promotion	une promotion
to	provide	fournir, offrir
to	provide credit arrangements	offrir des facilités de crédit
a	purchase	une acquisition, achat
to	purchase	acheter
	range	la gamme, la portée
to	reach	atteindre
to	recall products	retirer des produits de la vente
to	recruit	recruter, enroller
to	reduce	diminuer, réduire

a	reduction	une réduction, une baisse
	refund	le remboursement
to	refund	rembourser
the	report	le rapport
	reporting	le rapport, les rapports, reporting
	responsibility	la responsabilité
the	result	le résultat
the	retailer	le détaillant
	revenue	les recettes
the	rise	la hausse, une augmentation
to	rise	monter, augmenter, se lever
the	risk	le risque, le péril
a	salary	un salaire
	sales	soldes
to	ship	expédier
	when the sales are on	au moment des soldes
a	sample	un échantillon
a	schedule	un horaire, un planning
to	sell	vendre
a	seller	un vendeur
	solvent	solvable
	insolvent	insolvable
	in full settlement	pour solde de tout compte
a	stock	un stock, une réserve
to	stock up	renouveler le stock

to	subsidize	subventionner
to	succeed	réussir
	supply	offre
the	support	le soutien, un appui
a	survey	une enquête
	takeover	le rachat d'entreprise
	target market	le marché cible
a	trademark	une marque
	tax	impôt
	team building	renforcement d'équipe
a	think tank	une laboratoire d'idées, un groupe de réflexion
	transport	le transport
	trade	le commerce
the	trade register	le registre de commerce
a	trade show	une exposition commerciale
a	trade union	un syndicat
a	trend	une tendance
the	turnover	le renouvellement, la rotation
the	turnover (accounting)	le chiffre d'affaires
an	unfair competition	une concurrence déloyale
	value for money	rapport qualité-prix
to	violate a contract	violer un contrat, rompre un contrat
a	wage scale	une échelle des salaires
a	warehouse	un entrepôt
to	win	gagner

a	win-win game	un jeu gagnant-gagnant
	within 5 days	dans un délai de 5 jours

Bank and money

an	(account) overdraft	un découvert
	account	compte
to	apply for a loan	demander un prêt
to	ask for security	demander une garantie
an	ATM (automated Teller Machine, US), cash dispenser	un distributeur automatique
to	audit an account	vérifier un compte
a	balance	un solde (d'un compte bancaire)
a	bank	une banque
a	bank account	un compte bancaire
	bank card, ATM card (US)	carte bancaire
	bank cashier	caissière, caissier
	bank clerk	employé de banque
	bank manager	directeur de banque
a	bank note (GB), bill (US)	un billet de banque
	bank statement	relevé bancaire
	bank transfer	un virement bancaire
	banker	banquier
	banking	banque (organisation)
to	be in the red	être à découvert
to	borrow	emprunter
	building societies	association accès à la propriété

to	buy	acheter
to	buy on credit	acheter à crédit
	cash	du liquide
to	cash a cheque	toucher un chèque
to	change money (into euros)	changer de l'argent (en euros)
	cheap	bon marché, pas cher
a	cheque (GB), check (US)	un chèque
a	coin	une pièce de monnaie
	credit	crédit
	credit card	carte de crédit
	currency	devise, monnaie
a	current account (GB), checking account (US)	un compte courant
	debit, flow	débit
to	deposit money with a bank	déposer de l'argent en banque
	debt	dette
	discount rate	taux d'escompte, taux de remise
	exchange rate	taux de change
	expensive	cher
	financial markets	marchés financiers
	financier	financier
	foreign currency, foreign exchange	devise étrangère
	foreign exchange office, bureau de change (si)	bureau de change
to	give somebody credit	faire crédit à quelqu'un
to	grant a loan	accorder un prêt
	hard currency	devise forte

	interest	intérêt
	interest rate	taux d'intérêt
to	invest	investir
to	issue a cheque	libeller un chèque
	keep the change	gardez la monnaie
a	loan	un prêt, emprunt
to	make out a cheque	libeller un chèque
	money	monnaie, argent
	mortgage	prêt immobilier, hypothèque
to	open an account with	ouvrir un compte auprès de
	overdrawn account	compte à découvert
to	pay cash	payer en espèces
	pay slip	bulletin de salaire
	rate	taux
	real estate loan	prêt immobilier
	retail bank	banque de détail
to	save	économiser
	saving bank	caisse d'épargne
	secured credit	prêt garanti
to	speculate, gamble	jouer en bourse, spéculer
to	spend	dépenser
	statement (of account)	relevé de compte
	wages	salaire
to	withdraw	retirer (de l'argent)
to	write a check	faire un chèque

Chapter 4 – Eating and drinking

This chapter is about arranging to go for a drink or a meal.

Whether you're going out alone or with other people, you will probably do quite a bit of shopping and dining.

How To Order Food In France

So you travel to France and wanted to order food. This chapter will provide you with key "*French Ordering*" vocabulary, and the knowledge of how to request your meal. So here we go. There are different kinds or types of food restaurant in France. Try your best with the pronunciation, and if you're a real beginner at French, don't forget to carry a dictionary with you just in case!

Different type of restaurant in France

Café

They mainly serve coffee, of course, as well as tea, hot chocolate and light snacks such as sandwiches and toasts. Cafés typically feature a la carte style of dining, but daily specials and fixed prices can also be found. I usually like to order something small and enjoy the atmosphere outside. Sometimes you'll need to ask for the bill, other times it will just come out with your food.

Cafés are usually open from morning (roughly 7 am) until evening. Unlike some other establishments in France, cafés do not close mid-day.

Bistro

If you're in a hurry or just not looking for a real-sit down meal, bistros generally offer a casual atmosphere and are reasonably-priced. They are very popular destinations and so tend to get crowded, but beyond their cramped quarters, bistros offer a sampling of some of France's favorite culinary staples. They tend to be open only during meal hours, meaning from around 11:30 am- 2:00 pm for lunch and 7:30 pm- 11:00 pm for dinner.

Brasserie

Closely identifiable with pub restaurants, brasseries serve traditional French food, coffee and drinks at moderate prices. They offer a wider food selection than bistros and café. Plus, they are bustling and serving food all day long, from morning until late at night. As brasserie means "brewery" in French, you can expect a beer and wine selection that will satisfy true aficionados!

Bouchon

Bouchons usually tend to be meat-heavy dishes such as sausage, duck pâté and pork. Bouchons are known more for their convivial, lively atmospheres than refined haute cusine, but a hearty meal is guaranteed, usually accompanied by a glass of Beaujolais or Côtes-du-Rhône. Expect opening hours to coincide with meal times (see above).

Restaurant

Like bistros, restaurants are usually open only during meal hours (mentioned above), and many of them are not opened on Sundays or Mondays.

Auberge

Since auberges are often attached to bed and breakfasts or hotels. Auberges also offer accommodations to their visitors.

NOTE: This list is not exhaustive.

Restaurant Vocabulary

La carte (des vins)/ The menu (of wines)

À la carte: "From the Menu" type of dinning style when the diner selects individual

dishes (like the U.S)

Prix fixe: For this dining style, the diner selects from an already built menu; it usually

features several courses and is better priced than the "À la carte" option.

Un apéritif/ Pre-dinner drink, cocktail

L'entrée/ The appetizer

Le plat principal/ The main course

Le dessert/ The dessert

Le fromage/ The cheese course

Le digestif/ The digestive drink, after-dinner drink

…. du jour/ …. of the day

(Any dish followed by this phrase indicates it's a daily special, example: Menu du jour, Plat du jour)

Ordering Food Vocabulary

Est-ce que c'est possible d'avoir une table pour deux personnes ?/ Can I have a table for two? (Switch the word "deux" with any number you need)

Est-ce que vous avez une suggestion/une spécialité ?/ Do you have a suggestion/a specialty?

Est-ce qu'il y a un plat du jour ?/ Is there a daily special? (S-keel-E-Ah uhn plah do jewR)

Commander (Je suis prêt(e) à commander)/ To order (I am ready to order), note that you'll need the extra "e" if you're a woman. So, it's pronounced "prey" as a man and "phret" as a woman.

Je voudrais..., J'aimerais..., Je vais prendre.../ I would like…, I would love…, I will have… (all are appropriate)

Un morceau/ A piece

Une tranche/ A slice (of bread, meat, cake)

Une rondelle/ A slice (fruit, veggie)

Un verre de vin/ A glass of wine

Ce plat-là (requires you point)/ This dish here… (Very useful when you can't pronounce something)

Saignant, à point, bien cuit/ Rare, medium-rare, well done

Nous avons terminé/ We're finished eating

L'addition (s'il vous plaît)/ The bill (please)

Service (non) compris/ Tip (not) included

Avez-vous une table libre ?   / Do you have any spare tables? (polite)

Une table pour ..., s'il vous plaît / A table for ..., please

Deux	/ Two
Trois	/ Three
Quatre	/ Four
Je voudrais réserver une table.	I'd like to make a reservation.
À quel nom ?	/ In what name?

Au nom d'Alice   / In the name of Alice

Pour quand ?   / When for?

Ce soir à ... heures   / This evening at ... o'clock

Sept   / Seven

Huit   / Eight

Neuf   / Nine

Demain midi   / Tomorrow at noon

Demain à treize heures   / Tomorrow afternoon at one o'clock

Demain à quatorze heures   / Tomorrow afternoon at two o'clock

Demain à quinze heures   / Tomorrow afternoon at three o'clock

Pour combien de personnes ?   / For how many people?

J'ai réservé une table.   / I have a reservation.

Le menu, s'il vous plaît.   / The menu, please.

La carte des vins, s'il vous plaît.   / The wine menu, please.

Je suis végétarien(ne).   / I'm a vegetarian.

Je ne mange pas de viande.   / I don't eat meat.

Bon appétit !   / Enjoy your meal!

Vous prendrez autre chose ?   / Would you like anything else?

Vous prendrez un café ou un dessert ?   / Would you like any coffee or dessert?

L'addition, s'il vous plaît. / The bill, please.

Puis-je payer par carte ? / Can I pay by card?

C'était délicieux. / That was delicious.

C'était parfait. / That was delicious. (literally: that was perfect)

Entrées / Starters

Soupe / Soup

Soupe de poisson / Fish soup

Soupe de légumes / Vegetable soup

Soupe de tomate / Tomato soup

Crudités / Selection of raw vegetables

Assiette de charcuterie / Selection of cooked meats

Fruits de mer / Selection of seafood

Salade niçoise / Salad with tuna, peppers, and olives

Salade folle / Salad with foie gras

Plats principaux / Main courses

Steak frites / Steak and chips

Steak tartare / Raw steak

Bouillabaisse / Fish soup with pieces of fish

Desserts / Desserts

Sorbet / Sorbet

Crêpe / Pancake

Crème brûlée / Crème brûlée

Tarte aux pommes / Apple tart

Gâteau / Cake

En-cas / Snacks

Frites / Chips

Cacahuètes / Peanuts

Des chips / Crisps

Des olives / Olives

Viennoiseries / Sweet pastries

Croissant / Croissant

Pain au chocolat / Pastry with chocolate

Pain aux raisins / Pastry with raisins

Here you go with a list of words and phrases that you should arm yourself with. And no matter how wasted you get, remember to always keep it classy!

But let's get started with food's names in French.

Food's names in French

Vegetables/Légumes:

Légumes / Vegetables (lay-guum)

Aspargus: l'asperge

Bean: le haricot (ah-ree-KOH)

Beet: la betterave

Bell pepper: le poivron

Broccoli: le brocoli

Cabbage: le chou

Carrot: la carotte

Cassava: le manioc

Cauliflower: le chou-fleur

Celery: le céleri

Chickpea: pois chiche

Courgette: la courgette

Eggplant: l'aubergine

Endive: l'endive (in France) and le chicon (found in Belgium)

Garlic: l'ail

Gherkin: le cornichon

Globe artichoke: l'artichaut

Leek: le poireau

Lentil: la lentille

Lettuce or latuca: la laitue

Maize: le maïs

Mushroom: le champignon

Nettle: l'ortie

Onion: l'oignon

Pea: le petit pois

Pepper (UK) or chili (US): le piment

Potato: la pomme de terre and la patate (colloquial)

Pumpkin: la citrouille

Shallot: l'échalote

Soya bean: le soja

Spinach: l'épinard

Squash: la courge

Tomato: la tomate

Turnip: le navet

Wasabi: le wasabi

Fruits / Fruits:

The pome fruits

Apple: la pomme

Chokeberry: l'aronia

Loquat: la nèfle du Japon

Medlar: la nèfle

Pear: la poire

Quince: le coing

Apricot: l'abricot

Cherry: la cerise

Plum: la prune

Peach: la pêche

Greengage: la reine-claude

Bramble fruits: les mûres

Blackberry: la mûre sauvage (fruit de la ronce commune, ronce des haies, ronce des bois, mûrier sauvage, mûrier des haies, mûrier de renard, aronce)

Raspberry: la framboise

The true berries are dominated by the family Ericaceae

Bearberry: le raisin d'ours

Bilberry or whortleberry: la myrtille (commune)

Blueberry: la myrtille

Cranberry: le cranberry, la canneberge or l'atoca

Lingonberry: l'airelle rouge

Strawberry (Fragaria) : l'arbourse

Other berries not in the Rosaceae or Ericaceae

Currant: la groseille

Elderberry: le sureau

Hackberry: micocoule

Mulberry: la mûre

Asian Fuits

Goumi: Goumi du Japon

Kiwifruit or Chinese gooseberry or kiwi: le kiwi

Persimmon (or Sharon Fruit): le kaki or la plaquemine

Meat /Viande:

If you want your joint with crackling, this should be no problem for your local butcher, but you may need to order it in advance.

Useful vocabulary:

Poulet – chicken (probably ex-layer, and the 'normal' age to buy one). Poulette – young chicken.

Coq – cockerel

Pintade – guinea fowl

Dinde – turkey

Volaille – fowl/poultry

Cuisses – thighs

Magret – breast

Carcasse – carcasse for making stocks and soup

Derivate products:

Saucisses – sausage

Jambon – ham

Lamb/ Agneau:

Gigot d'agneau – leg of lamb

Echine – shoulder

Côtes – chump

Collet – scrag (end)

Poitrine/poitrail – breast

Côtelette – chop, usually from the rack of lamb, where the British cutlet comes from

Jarret – can mean shank or shin

Selle d'agneau – saddle

Steaks:

• *Bifteck/steak* – steak

Bavette – undercut – from the skirt, textured with long muscle fibres

Filet – fillet

Faux-filet – same

Steak à hacher – used for steak tartare and steak haché. Steak haché looks like a burger, but is simply this high quality steak minced up and pressed together. It is usually freshly done, which is why people are happy to eat them rare. Not comparable to a beef hamburger.

Romsteak/rumsteak – rump steak

Aloyau – sirloin

Entrecôte – ribeye

Tournedos/filet mignon – tenderloin steak usually cut almost as high as it is wide basically a chunk of tender steak, usually served quite rare unless otherwise requested (see 'Steak Doneness'). You can get 'tournedos' of lamb, too.

Other beef:

Tête de veau – head

Langue de bœuf – beef tongue

Gîte (à la noix) – topside

Queue – tail

Cou – neck

Tranche – meaning 'slice', implies a steak of any meat other than beef

Filet/longue/aloyau – all words for loin. Loin chop is 'côte première'

Seafood :

Poisson – fish

Morue – cod

Homard – lobster

Queue – tail

Moules – mussels

Huîtres – oysters

Homard – lobster

Saumon – salmon

Thon – tuna

Dairy products :

Lait – milk

Fromage – cheese

Beurre – butter

French cheeses:

There is a large variety of French cheese. Let's check it out!

French cheeses can be divided into three categories:

- **pressed cheeses** (like most British cheeses)
- **soft cheeses**, such as Camembert
- **blue cheeses** to which can be added a number of hybrids or very individual cheeses

Cheese is traditionally made from three types of milk:

cow's milk

goat's milk

sheep's milk

Pressed cheese (Made of cow's milk):

Comté

Cantal

Emmental

Mimolette

Reblochon

Soft cheeses:

Brie

Camembert

Epoisses

Gaperon

Munster

Pont l'Evèque

Saint Nectaire

Blue cheese:

Bleu de Bresse

Bleu des Causses

Bleu de Gex

Fourme d'Ambert

Roquefort

Drinks:

Eau gazeuse – Sparkling water

Jus – Juice

Café – Coffee

Vin – Wine

Bière – Beer

Rhum – Rhum

Thé – Tea

Whisky – Whisky

Food Preparation & Creation:

À la vapeur: Steamed

À l'étouffée: Stewed

Au four: Baked

En daube: In a stew

Bouilli: Boiled

Fondu: Melted

Fumé: Smoked

Haché: Minced (ground)

Grillé: Grilled

Frit: Fried

Dialog in the restaurant :

Arriving at the Restaurant

If you want to eat at a little café or a brewery, you should come and go. If you want a seat inside, choose the restaurant. A waiter will ask you how many people are in your party. In France, fancy restaurants typically require a reservation for dinner. I would advise calling a day in advance. Keep in mind that extremely popular restaurants are routinely booked days in advance. If that's the case, then you should search elsewhere or make a reservation for the next day.

Basic phrases:

Hello/Evening, a table for one person/two people, please. /Bonjour/Bonsoir, une table pour une personne/deux personnes, je vous prie. (uun TAHBL poor uun/deu pehr-SOHN zhuh voo PREE) /

Do you have a table near the window, please? /Avez-vous une table près de la fenêtre, s'il vous plaît ? (Ah-vay voo oohn tahbl-uh pray de lah fuhn-ehtr-uh, seel voo pleh?)

There are no more seats free?/ Il n'y a plus de table disponible ? (ill nia pluh deu tabl deesponeebl)

Menu

Can I look at the menu, please ?/ Puis-je avoir le menu ? (PWEEZH ah-VWAHR luh muh-NUU?)

Is there a local speciality?/ Y a-t-il une spécialité locale ? (yah-TEEL uun spay-see-ah-lee-TAY loh-KAHL?)

Is there a house speciality?/ Quelle est la spécialité de la maison ? (KELL eh lah spay-see-ah-lee-TAY duh lah meh-ZOHNG?)

What are today's specials?/ Quels sont les plats du jour, s'il vous plaît ? (Kell sohn lay plah doo jour, seel voo pleh?)

Do you have fixed-price menus?/ Avez-vous des menus à prix fixes ? (Ah-vay voo day meh-noo ah pree feex?)

Do you have a menu in English?/ Avez-vous un menu en anglais ? (Ah-vay voo unh meh-noo ahn ahn-glay?)

Is it possible to order take out?/ Est-ce possible de prendre des plats à emporter ? (Ess poh-see-bluh duh prawn-druh day plaugh ah ahm-pohr-teh?)

About your preferences:

I'm a vegetarian./ Je suis végétarien. (zhuh SWEE vay-zhay-tah-RYAHNG)

I don't eat meat./ Je ne mange pas de viande. (zhuh nuh mahnzh PAH duh veeond)

Je suis…/ I am…

I only eat kosher food./ Je ne mange que de la viande cachère. (zhuh nuh MAHNZH kuh duh lah VYAHND kah-SHEHR)

Ordering

I'll have (x), please/I'd like (x), please: Je prendrai (Name x), s'il vous plaît/Je voudrais (x), s'il vous plaît (Zhuh prahn-dreh (x), seel voo pleh/Zhuh voo-dreh (x), seel voo pleh)

I didn't order this. I had (x item): Je n'ai pas commandé ça. J'ai pris (Name x) (Zhuh n'ay pah koh-mahn-day sah. Zhay pree (x)

Can we have salt and pepper please?/ Du sel et du poivre, s'il vous plaît. (Doo sehl eh doo pwahv-ruh, seel voo pleh?)

May I have a bottle of _____?/ Puis-je avoir une bouteille de _____? (pweezh ah-VWAHR uun boo-TEYY duh _____?)

May I have some _____?/ Puis-je avoir du _____? (pweezh ah-VWAHR duu)

Excuse me, waiter? (getting attention of server)/ S'il vous plaît?

If you want something more or if you want to order something else:

I want _____./ Je voudrais _____. (zhuh voo-DREH _____)

I want a dish containing _____./ Je voudrais un plat avec _____. (zhuh voo-DREH ung plah ah-VEK _____)

May I have a glass of _____?/ Puis-je avoir un verre de _____? (pweezh ah-VWAHR ung VEHR duh _____?)

May I have a cup of _____?/ Puis-je avoir une tasse de _____? (pweezh ah-VWAHR uun TAHSS duh _____?)

Asking for the Check

Check, please?/ L'addition, s'il vous plaît ? (Lah-dee-sy-ohn, seel voo pleh?)

Do you take **credit cards**?/ Acceptez-vous les cartes de crédit ? (Ahk-septay voo lay cahrt de creh-dee?)

Can I get an official receipt, please?/ Je peux avoir une facture, s'il vous plaît? (Juh peuh ah-vwah uhn fak-tuh-ruh, seel voo pleh?)

Excuse me, but this bill isn't correct./ Excusez-moi, mais l'addition n'est pas correcte. (Ek-skew-zay mwah, may lah-dee-sy-ohn n'ay pah ko-rekt.)

Thank you, goodbye./ Merci, au revoir. (Mehr-si, oh ruh-vwah)

Leaving Tips

Once you are finished with your meal and are ready to leave, you'll need to ask for the tip. In France, servers are paid a regular wage and do not rely on tips. They won't make you feel rushed, tipping a euro is a symbol of "extremely great service", keep that in mind. Leaving a euro or two on the table is a super kind gesture for your server, but it's not required at all. That being said, it's up to you.

Phrases:

J'ai fini./ I'm finished.

C'était délicieux./ It was delicious.

Vous pouvez débarrasser la table./ Please clear the plates.

Vocabulary:

Breakfast: petit-déjeuner (ptee-day-zheu-NAY)

Lunch: déjeuner (day-zheu-NAY)

Dinner: dîner (dee-NAY)

Supper: souper (soo-PAY)

La carte: menu

Menu/s: (fixed-price) menu/s

Service compris/non compris: service tax included/not included (restaurants generally have "service compris")

Apéritifs: before-meal drinks

Entrées: starters

Plats: main dishes

Dessert: desserts

Fromages: cheeses (often presented along with dessert items)

Digestifs: after-dinner drinks

Viandes: meat dishes

Légumes: vegetables

Poissons et crustacés: fish and shellfish

Plats d'enfant: children's dishes

Plats végétariens: **vegetarian dishes**

Boissons: drinks/drink menu

(Carte de) vins: wine (menu)

Vins rouges: red wines

Vins blancs: white wines

Vin moussant: sparkling wine

Vins rosés: rose/blush wines

Eau minérale: mineral water

Eau pétillante: sparkling mineral water

Eau plate: still water

Carafe d'eau: pitcher of (tap) water

Jus: juice/s

Bière/s: beer/s

Café: espresso

Café allongé: espresso diluted with hot water

Café noisette: espresso with small dollop of milk

At the restaurant

English	French
The restaurant	Le restaurant
Would you like to eat?	Est-ce que tu veux manger ?
Yes, with pleasure	Oui, je veux bien
To eat	Manger
Where can we eat?	Où pouvons-nous manger ?
Where can we have lunch?	Où pouvons-nous prendre le déjeuner ?
Dinner	Le dîner
Breakfast	Le petit-déjeuner

English	French
Excuse me!	S'il vous plaît !
The menu, please	Le menu, s'il vous plaît !
Here is the menu	Voilà le menu !
What do you prefer to eat? Meat or fish?	Qu'est-ce que tu préfères manger, de la viande ou du poisson ?
With rice	Avec du riz
With pasta	Avec des pâtes
Potatoes	Des pommes de terre
Vegetables	Des légumes
Scrambled eggs – fried eggs - or a boiled egg	Des oeufs brouillés - sur le plat - ou à la coque
Bread	Du pain
Butter	Du beurre
Salad	Une salade
Dessert	Un dessert
Fruit	Des fruits
Can I have a knife, please?	Puis-je avoir un couteau s'il vous plaît ?
Yes, I'll bring it to you right away	Oui, je vous l'apporte tout de suite
A knife	Un couteau
A fork	Une fourchette
A spoon	Une cuillère

English	French
Is it a warm dish?	Est-ce que c'est un plat chaud ?
Yes, very hot also!	Oui, et très épicé également !
Warm	Chaud
Cold	Froid
Hot	Epicé
I'll have fish	Je vais prendre du poisson !
Me too	Moi aussi

Bar

English	French
The bar	Le bar
Would you like to have a drink?	Tu veux boire quelque chose ?
To drink	Boire
Glass	Verre
With pleasure	Avec plaisir
What would you like?	Qu'est-ce que tu prends ?
What's on offer?	Qu'est-ce qu'il y a à boire ?
There is water or fruit juices	Il y a de l'eau ou des jus de fruits
Water	Eau
Can you add some ice cubes, please?	Pouvez-vous ajouter des glaçons s'il vous plaît ?
Ice cubes	Des glaçons

English	French
Chocolate	Du chocolat
Milk	Du lait
Tea	Du thé
Coffee	Du café
With sugar	Avec du sucre
With cream	Avec de la crème
Wine	Du vin
Beer	De la bière
A tea please	Un thé s'il vous plaît
A beer please	Une bière s'il vous plaît
Tea	Du thé

Mc Donald's

This part is necessary because sometimes you won't feel like eating and having a real dinner or lunch; sometimes you won't feel like eating light at all. That's why when you'll be in a hurry you'll simply go to Mc Donald's.

The French don't say Mc Donald, they simply call it "McDo".

« On se fait un petit McDo ? » (On sfay enh ptee McDo ?) has no real translation in English but it can be "Do you want to go to McDo?".

Ordering in McDo

The simplest way to order something is to say **bonjour** + the name of the thing you want + **s'il vous plaît.** You don't need to bother saying introductory stuff like "**je voudrais**".

The meals at McDonalds are called **trios** in French. **Le trio Big Mac** is the Big Mac combo.

When ordering in French, a little **bonjour, je voudrais….** is perfectly correct, but let's give you some more frequently used ways to order.

Bonjour, le trio Big Mac, s'il vous plaît.

Hello, the Big Mac combo, please.

If you want to precede the name of what you want by introductory words, you can use **"je vais prendre"**.

Bonjour, je vais prendre le trio Big Mac, s'il vous plaît.

Hello, I'll take the Big Mac combo, please.

But it's also fine if you want to order food by saying their number at McDo.

Bonjour, je vais prendre le numéro 6, s'il vous plaît.

Hello, I'll take number 6, please.

Sometimes people say **"ça va être"** instead.

Bonjour, ça va être le trio Big Mac.

Hello, [it's going to be] the Big Mac combo.

For **"je vais prendre"**. The **re** ending is often dropped so that **prendre** sounds like **prende**.

At McDonalds, you'll be asked:

C'est pour ici ou pour emporter ? Is it for here or to go?

You can answer **(c'est) pour ici** or simply **(c'est) pour emporter**.

Chapter 5 – Accommodation

Hotels

Hotels in France are inspected and rated with respect to their level of comfort, amenities, and quality of service. French hotels are approved and checked by official authorities, and classified into seven categories by the government: no star, 1*, 2*, 3*, 4*, 5* and Palaces. Hotel rates are also unregulated and usually there is an extra charge for breakfast. Many hotels usually have their own restaurant.

Here is a Top 10 of hotels in France:

La Réserve Paris - Hotel and Spa (Paris, France)

Hôtel Fabric (Paris, France)

Hôtel Monge (Paris, France)

Mandarin Oriental (Paris, France)

La Maison Favart (Paris, France)

Hôtel Le Six (Paris, France)

Le Bristol (Paris, France)

Hôtel Keppler (Paris, France)

Hôtel Saint Paul Rive Gauche (Paris, France)

Grand Hôtel des Alpes (Chamonix, France)

Bookings

There are different ways to book in France. Reservations can be made by letter, fax, email, internet, phone, etc. Most of the time, a deposit should be sent to the hotel. Your booking, room rate and receipt of deposit should be confirmed in writing, by the hotelier. To book your room, ask directly at booking agents for the hotel's chain.

Phrases for booking:

Do you have a room available?/ Avez-vous une chambre libre ?

How much is it for a night?/ Quel est le prix d'une nuit ?

Do you have any rooms available (for the 5th June)?/ Avez-vous des chambres disponibles (pour le 5 juin) ?

OK, can I reserve for tonight?/ C'est bon, est-ce que je peux réserver pour ce soir ?

I would like a room on the third floor, if possible./ Je voudrais une chambre au troisième étage, si possible.

I'd like a double room for three nights./ J'aimerais une chambre double pour trois nuits.

How much does it cost per day?/ Combien ça coûte par jour ?

How much is full board?/ Combien coûte la pension complète ?

How much is half board?/ Combien coûte la demi-pension ?

A room with (a) balcony/ Une chambre avec (un) balcon

Do you have a room with a balcony?/ Vous avez une chambre avec (un) balcon ?

A room that faces the courtyard/ Une chambre qui donne sur la cour

I would like a room that faces the courtyard./ Je voudrais une chambre qui donne sur la cour.

A room that does not face the street/ Une chambre qui ne donne pas sur la rue

We prefer a room that does not face the street./ Nous préférons une chambre qui ne donne pas sur la rue.

A non-smoking room/ Une chambre non-fumeur

This is a non-smoking room./ C'est une chambre non-fumeur.

Is there a bathroom in the room?/ Y a-t-il une salle de bain avec la chambre ?

Would you prefer two single beds?/ Préférez-vous deux lits une personne ?

Do you wish to have a twin room?/ Souhaitez-vous une chambre double ?

A room with bathtub – with balcony – with shower/ Une chambre avec bain - avec balcon - avec douche

Bed and breakfast/ Chambre avec petit-déjeuner

I would like to see the room first./ Je voudrais voir la chambre d'abord s'il vous plaît.

Yes, of course./ Oui bien sûr !

Thank you, the room is very nice./ Merci, la chambre est très bien.

It's a bit too much for me, thank you./ C'est un peu trop cher pour moi, merci.

Could you take care of my luggage, please?/ Pouvez-vous vous occuper de mes bagages, s'il vous plaît ?

Where is my room, please?/ Où se trouve ma chambre s'il vous plaît ?

It is on the first floor./ Elle est au premier étage.

Is there a lift?/ Est-ce qu'il y a un ascenseur ?

The elevator is on your left./ L'ascenseur est sur votre gauche.

The elevator is on your right./ L'ascenseur est sur votre droite.

Where is the laundry room, please?/ Où se trouve la blanchisserie, s'il vous plaît ?

It is on the ground floor./ Elle est au rez-de-chaussée.

Car parking space/ Parking pour les voitures

Let's meet in the meeting room./ On se retrouve dans la salle de réunion.

Meeting room/ La salle de réunion

The swimming pool is heated./ La piscine est chauffée.

Please, wake me up at seven am./ Réveillez-moi à sept heures, s'il vous plaît.

The key, please./ La clé, s'il vous plaît.

The pass, please./ Le pass, s'il vous plaît.

Are there any messages for me?/ Est-ce qu'il y a des messages pour moi ?

Yes, here you are./ Oui, les voilà.

No, we didn't receive anything for you./ Non, vous n'avez rien reçu.

Could you bring me a bottle of champagne to my room?/ Pouvez-vous apporter une bouteille de champagne dans ma chambre ?

I need some paper / envelopes / stamps./ J'ai besoin de feuilles / enveloppe / timbres.

My luggage is in the boot / trunk./ Mes bagages sont dans le coffre.

I have a reservation for tonight./ J'ai une réservation pour ce soir.

Is breakfast included?/ Le petit déjeuné est-il inclu ?

Could you get my bill ready please?/ Pouvez-vous me préparer la note s'il vous plaît ?

Questions about the hotel's restaurant schedule:

A quelle heure le restaurant ouvre-t-il ?/ferme-t-il ?/ What time does the restaurant open/close?

A quelle heure servez-vous le petit déjeuner/le déjeuner/le dîner ?/ What time do you serve breakfast/lunch/dinner?

Leaving the hotel :

Je partirai le matin./ I'll be leaving tomorrow morning.

Je partirai demain après-midi/soir./ I'll be leaving tomorrow afternoon/night.

Pouvez-vous me dire à quoi correspond ce frais ?/ Could you tell me what this charge is for?

Paying the bill :

Vous prenez les cartes bancaires ?/ Do you take credit cards?

Où puis-je faire de la monnaie ?/ Where can I get some change?

Pouvez-vous me faire de la monnaie, s'il vous plaît ?/ Please can you give me some change?

Nous pouvons vous en faire. Combien voulez-vous changer ?/ We can make some for you, how much would you like?

Useful vocabulary :

The hotel/ L'hôtel

Apartment/ Appartement

Welcome!/ Bienvenue !

Do not distub/ Ne pas déranger

Fire escape/ Escaliers de secours

Fire exit/ Sortie de secours

Accommodation/ Logement

Swimming pool/ La piscine

Ground floor/ Rez-de-chaussée

Bedroom/ Chambre

Dry cleaner's/ Pressing

Hair salon/ Salon de coiffure

A single room/ Une chambre individuelle

A double room/ Une chambre double

A single bed/ Un lit simple

A doubled bed/ Un lit double

Double-bedded room/ Une chambre avec un lit double

Beds/ Lits jumeaux

A twin-bedded room/ Une chambre avec des lits jumeaux

A room with en suite bathroom/ Une chambre avec salle de bain

Booking/ Une réservation

Luggage/ Un bagage

Life/ Un ascenseur

First (second/third/fourth) floor/ Premier (deuxième/troisième/quatrième) étage

Key/ La clef

Key card/ La carte magnétique

Receipt/ Le reçu, la facture

Bill/ L'addition

Reception/ La réception

Receptionist/ Le/la réceptionniste

Restaurant/ Le restaurant

Bar/ Le bar

Dining room/ Salle de restaurant

Lounge/ Le salon

Waiter/waitress/ Le serveur/la serveuse

Chambermaid/ Femme de chambre

Bellboy/ Un bagagiste

Parking lot attendant/ Gardien de parking

Manager/ Le directeur

Room service/ Service de chambre

Laundry service/ La laverie

To iron/ Repasser

To wash/ Laver

Stairs/ Les escaliers

To pay a deposit or down payment/ Payer un dépôt ou verser un accompte

Refund/ Un remboursement

A tip/ Un pourboire

Camping

air bed		un matelas pneumatique
an	air pump	un gonfleur
	axe [ax : US]	une hache
a	backpack (knapsack, packsack)	un sac à dos
a	billycan	une gamelle
	boots	bottes
a	camp	un camp
to	camp	camper
	camp bed	lit de camp
	camper	campeur
a	campervan	un camping car
	campfire	feu de camp
	campground	terrain de camping
	camping stove	camping-gaz, réchaud
	campsite	terrain de camping
	campstool	siège pliant
a	caravan	une caravane
	caravan site	terrain de caravaning
	compass	boussole
	firewood	bois de chauffage

	flashlight	lampe de poche
	flask	gourde
a	fly sheet	un double toit, une moustiquaire
	forest	bois, forêt
	grill	grill
	ground sheet	tapis de sol
	hammock	hammac
	hatchet	hachette
	hook	crochet
	ice cooler	glacière
	insect repellent	insectifuge
	lamp	lampe
	lantern	lanterne
	mallet	maillet
	matches	allumettes
	map	carte
a	mobile home	mobile-home
	outdoors	en plein air
	raincoat	imperméable
	rope	corde
	sleeping bag	sac de couchage
	stake	piquet
a	tent	tente
	pegs	piquets

a	penknife		canif
	pitch a tent		planter une tente
	the showers		les douches
to	take down a tent		démonter une tente
	thermos		thermos
	toilet block		les sanitaires
	torch		lampe de poche
	trailer		caravane
	trap		piège
	water bottle		bouteille d'eau

Chapter 6 – Shopping

Different types of shops:

Grand magasin/ Department store

Centre commercial/ Shopping centre

Zone commerciale/ Shopping precinct

Magasin de chaussures/ Shoe store

Magasin de vêtements/ Clothes store

Magasin de disques/ Record store

Épicerie/ Grocery store

Boulangerie/ Bakery

Librairie/ Bookshop

Bureau de poste/ Post office

Pâtisserie/ Cake shop

Phrases about shopping :

Je vais faire du shopping samedi. – I am going shopping on Saturday.

Puis-je vous aider ? – Can I help you?

Vous cherchez quelque chose en particulier ? – Are you looking for something in particular?

Je cherche… - I am looking for…

Un pull vert - A green sweater

Un cadeau - A present

Quelque chose de moins cher - Something cheaper

Je regarde tout simplement. – I am just looking.

C'est combien ? – How much is it?

Cher - Expensive

Bon marché - Cheap

Comptant / Espèce / Liquide – Cash

Vendeur / Vendeuse – Sales assistant (m/f)

Caissier / Caissière – Cashier (m/f)

Ticket de caisse - Receipt

Puis-je avoir un sac ? – Can I have a bag?

Shopping for clothes

Y a-t-il des soldes ? – Do you have any sales on?

Est-ce que cette jupe est en solde ? – Is this skirt in the sale?

J'aime celui/celle-ci ! – I like this (m/f) one!

Je cherche ce jean en taille 40. – I am looking for these jeans in a size 40.

Avez-vous cette chemise en taille 12 ? – Do you have this shirt in a size 12?

Avez-vous cette robe en d'autres couleurs ? – Do you have this dress in other colours?

Cette couleur ne me va pas très bien. – This colour doesn't suit me.

Je voudrais la voir en noir. – I would like to see it in black.

Je vais essayer ce pull. – I am going to try on this sweater.

Où sont les cabines ? – Where are the changing rooms?

C'est trop… - It is too…

Serré - Tight

Court - Short

Large - Big

Ce pull me plaît beaucoup. – I really like this sweater.

J'adore cette robe. Je la prends. – I love this dress. I will take it!

J'ai envie d'acheter ces chaussures mais je ne peux pas me le permettre. – I want to buy these shoes but they are too expensive.

Puis-je payer/régler par carte de crédit ? – Can I pay by credit card?

Quelle est votre politique pour les remboursements ? – What is your returns policy?

Puis-je retourner cet article ? – Can I return this item?

Je voudrais échanger cette chemise pour une autre taille, s'il vous plaît. – I would like to exchange this shirt for one in another size please.

Browsing and Looking for Specific Items

A sales clerk, or vendeur, vendeuse, might ask you if you need help.

Est-ce que je peux vous aider ?

Or if you're looking for something in particular./ Vous cherchez quelque chose en particulier ?

Paying and Asking for Prices

How much is it?/ C'est combien ?/ Combien ça coûte ?

Can I pay by card?/ Est-ce que je peux payer par carte bancaire ?/ Je peux régler par carte ?

I'm going to pay in cash./ Je vais payer en liquide.

I'm going to check out, I'm going to the cash register./ Je vais à la caisse.

Can I have a bag?/ Est-ce que je peux avoir un sac ?

How to say that you're just looking:

Non merci, je ne fais que regarder. (No thank you, I'm only looking.)/ Non merci, je regarde tout simplement. (No thank you, I'm simply looking.)

Or that you're looking for a green sweater./ Oui, je cherche un pull vert.

I need to buy a present for a friend./ Je dois trouver un cadeau pour un ami.

Sizes and Colors

Do you have this in a large?/ Est-ce que vous l'avez en L ?

I'm looking for these jeans in a 36./ Je cherche ce jean en taille 36.

Do you have other sizes?/ Est-ce que vous avez d'autres tailles ?

I would like to see this dress but in black./ Je voudrais voir cette robe mais en noir.

Do you have this in other colors?/ Est-ce que vous l'avez en d'autres couleurs ?

Trying Things On

Where are the dressing rooms?/ Où sont les cabines ?

Is there a mirror?/ Est-ce qu'il y a un miroir ?

I'm going to try on these pants./ Je vais essayer ce pantalon.

It's too tight!/ C'est trop serré !

It's a bit short, don't you think?/ C'est un peu court, n'est-ce pas ?

That's way too big on you./ C'est beaucoup trop large pour vous.

Returns and Refunds

What's your return policy?/ Quelle est votre politique pour les remboursements ?

I would like to exchange this for another size, please./ Je voudrais échanger ceci pour une autre taille, s'il vous plaît.

I would like to return this watch./ Je voudrais retourner cette montre.

Can I be reimbursed in cash?/ Je pourrais être remboursé(e) en liquide ?

Remember to check the hours of the store you're going to and see if they're open during the weekend. While some stores are open on Sundays, especially in certain neighborhoods of Paris, the majority aren't open. Opening hours are often extended during the sales and during the Christmas holidays.

What time do you close?/ Vous fermez à quelle heure ?

Are you open on Sundays?/ Vous êtes ouvert les dimanches ?

At the supermarket

If you ever go to France, one of the things you will have to do on your own is buy food, from le supermarché (supermarket) or the local épicerie (food store).

The first useful sentence you probably should learn is "excusez-moi" ("excuse me"), followed by "avez-vous…?" ("do you have…?"), and then you say the name of the product or food you want to buy.

For example, if it's le lait (milk), you would say: "avez-vous du lait ?" ("do you have milk?")

If you are looking for, say, tomatoes, you would say: "avez-vous des tomates ?"

The first thing you probably want to use, when entering a supermarket, is either un caddie (a shopping cart), or just un panier (a basket), if you plan to buy only a few items.

If you can't find the shopping carts, you can politely ask:

"Où sont les caddies, s'il vous plaît ?"/ Where are the shopping carts, please?

Once inside, you can ask for a specific aisle: "Où est le rayon… ?"/ Where is the… aisle?

Phrase: Où est le rayon fruits et légumes, s'il vous plaît ?/ Where is the fruits and vegetables aisle, please?

You will probably also have to remember how to say such things as "poisson frais" ("fresh fish"), "viande fraîche" ("fresh meat"), "le pain" ("bread"), "l'huile d'olive" ("olive oil"), "les œufs" ("eggs"), "les pommes" ("apples"), "les pommes de terre" ("potatoes"), "les surgelés" ("frozen food"), etc.

Quel fruit détestez/préférez-vous le plus ? /What fruit do you hate/like the most?

Once you're done with your shopping, the caissier or caissière (male or female cashier) would normally ask you: "Ce sera tout ?"/ "Would that be all?"

Paying:

If yes, then you will either have the option of paying avec du liquide (with cash) or par carte bancaire (with a bank card.)

Phrases :

Prenez-vous les cartes bancaires ?/ Do you accept credit cards ?

French Supermarket Vocabulary

Here you will find a complete list of French grocery store vocabulary words. You'll find this list extremely useful if you're shopping in France and cannot find what you're looking for in the grocery store

le supermarché/ supermarket/grocery store

le caddie/ trolley/shopping cart

le panier/ shopping basket

les provisions/ groceries

les promotions/ offers/sales

le caissier/ cashier

le tapis roulant/ conveyer belt

l'étagère/ shelf

la caisse/ checkout

l'allée/ aisle

la caisse/ till/cash register

le sac à provisions/ shopping bag

le code-barres/ bar code

le lecteur optique/ scanner

la crèmerie/ dairy section

la boulangerie/ bakery

les céréales/ cereals

les converves/ canned/tinned food

la confiserie/ confectionary/sweets section

les légumes/ vegetables

la viande et volaille/ meat and poultry

les fruits/ fruits

le poisson/ fish

la charcuterie/ deli

les produits surgelés/ frozen food

les boissons/ beverages

les plats cuisinés/ instant meals

les produits d'entretien/ household (cleaning) products

les articles de toilette/ toiletries

les articles pour bébé/ baby section

la nourriture pour animaux/ pet food

l'électroménager/ electrical goods

les magazines/revues/ magazines

Chapter 7 – Hair Salon

At the salon

Haircut - Useful Phrases:

French spelling is really different from English. Use the pronunciation guide in italics to say these phrases. The oo is like the oo in moon and the zhe is like the s in pleasure.

Un fondu de nuque (uhn fon-doo duh nuke)/ To shave your neck

Les pattes courtes (ou juste désépaissies) (lay pat court (day-zah-pez-ee)/ Short sideburns (or thinned)

Gardez la longueur mais coupez le haut. (Gar-day lah loh-ger may coop-ay luh oh)/ Keep the length please, but cut the top.

Court partout (Coor par too)/ Short all over

Dying/Coloring your hair:

• Can you colour my hair? = Est-ce que vous pouvez faire la couleur ? (es-sah-kuh voo poo-vay fair lah coo-lar)

• Could you make my colour darker? = Est-ce que vous pouvez faire la couleur plus foncée ? (es-sah-kuh voo poo-vay fair lah coo-lar ploo fon-say)

• Could you make my colour lighter? = Est-ce que vous pouvez faire la couleur plus claire ? (es-sah-kuh voo poo-vay fair lah coo-lar ploo klay-r)

Between two colours = Entre deux couleurs (awn-tr duh coo-lar)

Yes = oui (wee) No = non (no)

Please = s'il vous plaît (see voo play)

• I would like my colour to be lighter/darker. = Je veux que ma couleur soit plus claire (foncée). (Zhe ver kuh mah coo-lar swah ploo klair (fon-see))

• I would like my roots coloured. = Je veux teindre mes racines. (Zhe ver tandr may ras-seen)

• Light perm = Permanente souple (payr-man-awnt soupl)

• May I have a full head of highlights? = Je veux des mèches sur toute la tête or Est-ce que je peut avoir des mèches partout? (Zhe ver day mesh sir toot lah tet)

• Tight perm = Permanente soutenue (payr-man-awnt soo teh-noo)

• Trim the ends = Coupez les pointes (ay-pwent-ay luh bah)

• Layered/to thin out = dégradez/enlevez un peu d'épaisseur (day-grah-day on-lev-ay)

Haircut: *une coupe*

Shampoo: le shampooing

Colouring and highlights: les couleurs et mèches

Set or styling: la mise en pli

Perm: la permanente

Haircare and treatments: les soins et traitements

A blow-dry or straightening: le brushing

Top salon: un coiffeur haut de gamme

Local salon: coiffeur de quartier

Basic French hair terms:

Your hair: vos cheveux (always masculine, plural)

Fine: fins

Thick: épais

Oily: gras

Dry: secs

Mixed: mixtes

Normal: normaux

Curly: bouclés

Frizzy: frisés

Smooth: lisses

Damaged: abîmés

Dyed: colorés

Permed: permanentés

Dandruff: pellicules

Cowlick: un épi

A lock of hair: une mèche

French terms for getting a haircut:

Short or long: la coupe courte ou longue

Layered: en dégradé

Blunt cut: au carré

Clean cut/well-defined: bien dégagée

Asymmetrical: asymétrique

Square tapered: style carré effilé

Layered on top: dégradé sur le dessus

Short, layered look: une coupe courte tout en dégradé

Short 'windblown' layered look: dégradé déstructuré

'Just out of bed' look: indiscipliné

Highlights or streaks: les mèches

Hair weaving or foiling: balayage

Bangs: une frange

Hair part: une raie

Hair ends: les pointes

Hair treatments and styling in French

Hair conditioner: une crème ou après-shampooing

Deep-conditioning hair mask: un masque capillaire

Anti-dandruff treatment: un traitement antipelliculaire

Hair loss treatment: un traitement antichute

Blow dry for a curly look: un brushing bouclé

Slightly turned up at the ends: un brushing avec un léger mouvement sur les pointes

Straightened: un brushing raide

Hairdryer: un sèche-cheveux

Billing:

How much will this cost? = Combien est-ce que ça coûte ? (Comb-bee-en es-sah-kah sah koot?)

At the barber:

French hair terms for men

Sideburns: les pattes

Beard: une barbe

Clippers: une tondeuse

Crew cut: coupe en brosse

Nape of the neck: la nuque

Hairline: l'implantation

Common dialog in the hair salon/Barber:

What can I do for you today? *Qu'est-ce que je vous fais aujourd'hui ?*

I cut this out of a magazine. Do you think it would suit me? *J'ai découpé ça dans un magazine. Vous pensez que ça m'irait ?*

I've come to have the colour touched up. *Je viens pour me refaire ma couleur.*

I just want the roots redone. *Je veux seulement une coloration des racines.*

I haven't made up my mind about the colour – a permanent or semi-permanent colour. *J'hésite pour la couleur – une couleur permanente ou une simple coloration.*

Can you give me highlights? *Vous pouvez me faire des mèches ?*

Is that possible with my hair type? *C'est possible avec mon type de cheveux ?*

Would you prefer it to dry naturally or shall I blow-dry it? *Préférez-vous un séchage naturel ou un brushing ?*

Perhaps just tapered or layered? *Peut-être un simple effilage ou encore un dégradé ?*

What's the difference? Tapering lightens the cut by thinning, with layering you get a more structured, shorter cut. *Quelle est la différence ? Un effilage allège la coupe en enlevant la masse, avec un dégradé, vous avez une coupe plus structurée avec des mèches plus courtes.*

To avoid frizziness, I could lift the roots. *Pour ne pas friser, je peux vous faire un décollement des racines.*

Shall I cut it short and towel dry? *Je vous fais une coupe courte avec un séchage à la serviette ?*

Should I set your hair? *Je vous fais une mise en pli ?*

Could you take a bit more off at the nape/ the sides? *Vous pouvez diminuer sur la nuque / sur les pattes ?*

It's too puffed up. Could you flatten it down a bit? *C'est trop gonflé, vous pouvez aplatir un peu ?*

A touch of gel to finish off? *Un soupçon de gel pour finir le tout ?*

Chapter 8 – Rent and Car driving

ROUTES / ROADS's Vocabulary

Whether you are moving there or just visiting on holiday, be sure to learn this list of key phrases relating to hiring a car in France, French road signs and other key phrases relating to driving in France.

La route principale/ the main road

Le périphérique/ a bypass

Un cul-de-sac/ a dead-end street

Un péage/ a toll road

Une autoroute/ a motorway (Am. freeway)

Une nationale/ an A-road (Am. highway)

Une piste cyclable/ a cycle lane/a cycleway

Une route/ a road (between towns)

Une route à quatre voies/ a dual carriageway (Am. divided highway)

Une route à sens unique/ a one-way street

Une route régionale/ a B-road (Am. secondary road)

Une voie/ a lane

Car Rentals

Conditions you should know:

In France, to be able to rent a car, you must be : 21 years, have a 1 year old license, be able to present proof of identity (passport, identity card) to the tenant and also provide the original copy of your driver's license.

Here are the key car rental agencies in France : Europcar, Avis, Hertz, Sixt, Rentacar

Hire car glossary

I would like to rent a car./ Je voudrais louer une voiture.

How much is it per day?/ C'est combien par jour ?

Is insurance included in the price?/ Est-ce que l'assurance est comprise ?

I made a booking last month./ J'ai fait une réservation le mois dernier.

I need a transfer from the city to the airport./ J'ai besoin d'un transfert ville-aéroport.

I need a 4×4 for the mountains./ Il me faut un 4×4 (quatre par quatre or 'cat-cat' phonetically) pour la montagne.

Do you have a camper-van available in Provence next week?/ Avez-vous un camping-car disponible en Provence la semaine prochaine ?

Is it possible to have a car with a driver?/ Est-ce possible d'avoir une voiture avec chauffeur ?

I would like to modify/change an existing reservation./ Je voudrais modifier une réservation existante.

I have to cancel my reservation./ Je dois annuler ma réservation.

Where is your office?/ Où se trouve votre agence ?

Key words and phrases when driving:

Some essential French road signs

Follow the signs./ Suivez les panneaux.

Agricultural vehicles have right of way./ Priorité aux véhicules agricoles.

You do not have right of way./ Vous n'avez pas la priorité.

Exit for vehicles./ Sortie véhicules

Parking prohibited./ Stationnement interdit.

Slow down (for our children)./ Ralentissez (pour nos enfants).

Exit/ Sortie

Give way/ Cédez le passage

One way/ Sens unique

Town centre/ Centre ville

Diversion/ Déviation

All exits must be kept clear./ Toutes les sorties doivent rester dégagées.

Railway station/ Gare SNCF

Narrow lanes/ Files étroites

Keep in lane./ Ne changez pas de file.

Get in lane./ Mettez-vous dans/sur la bonne file.

No overtaking./ Interdiction de doubler/dépasser.

Deliveries/ Livraisons

No loading or unloading./ Interdiction de charger ou de décharger.

Restricted parking zone/ Zone bleue

Pedestrian precinct/ Zone piétonnne/piétonnière

Traffic/ La circulation

A traffic jam/ Un embouteillage

Reminder of the speed limit./ Rappel de limitation de vitesse

An estate car/ Un break

A touring-car/ Une routière

Roundabout/ Rond-point

At the gas station:

La voiture n'a plus d'essence.	This car is out of gas.
Où est-ce qu'il y a une station-service près d'ici ?	Where is there a gas station near here?
Le plein, s'il vous plaît.	Fill it up, please.
Vingt litres, s'il vous plaît.	20 liters, please.
Cette voiture utilise de l'essence ordinaire.	This car uses regular gas.
Cette voiture utilise de l'essence sans plomb.	This car uses unleaded gas.
Cette voiture utilise du diesel.	This car uses diesel.
Est-ce que c'est la bonne route pour Paris ?	Is this the right road for Paris?
Voici mon permis de conduire.	Here is my driver's license.
Est-ce que je roulais trop rapidement ?	Was I driving too fast?

la location de voitures car rental

louer une voiture   to rent a car

réserver une voiture   reserve a car

prendre la voiture   to take / pick up the car

	to return the car
rendre la voiture	

Car's renting

J'aimerais louer une voiture, s'il vous plaît.	I'd like to rent a car please.
Avez-vous une voiture manuelle ?	Do you have a manual shift car?
Avez-vous une voiture automatique ?	Do you have an automatic (car)?
C'est combien pour louer par jour, s'il vous plaît ?	How much is it to rent per day, please?
C'est combien pour louer par semaine, s'il vous plaît ?	How much is it to rent per week, please?
Je voudrais....	I would like....
...une voiture compacte.	...a compact car.
...une voiture intermédiaire.	...a mid-sized car.
...une grosse voiture.	...a big car.
...une petite voiture.	...a small car.
...un quatre-quatre.	...a 4 x 4.
...un camion.	...a truck.
...une voiture luxe.	...a luxury car.
...une voiture hybride.	...a hybrid car.
...une voiture électrique.	...an electric car.

Vehicle parts:

Le frein	Brake
Le frein à main	Hand brake
Le siège conducteur	Driver seat
La ceinture de sécurité	Seat belt

Le klaxon	Horn
Le tableau de bord	Dashboard
Le clignotant	Indicator / blinker
Le phare	Headlight
Les feux de route (plein phare)	Full beam lights
Les feux de croisement	Dipped headlights
Le rétroviseur	Rearview mirror / side mirror
L'embrayage	Clutch
Le volant	Steering wheel
L'accélérateur (m)	Accelerator / Gas pedal
Un champignon	Accelerator (informal)
L'allumage (m)	Ignition system
La boîte de vitesses	Gear box
Le levier de vitesses	Gear stick
La boîte manuelle	Manual transmission / Stick shift
La transmission automatique	Automatic transmission
Le toit ouvrant	Sky-light
La décapotable, le cabriolet	Convertible
L'appui-tête (m)	Headrest
Le moteur	Motor
Le capot	Hood
Le coffre arrière	Rear boot
L'aile (f)	Wing
Le réservoir	Petrol/gas tank

De l'essence (f)	Gas / petrol
Du sans plomb (essence)	Unleaded gas
Du super (essence)	Premium gas
Le gasoil, gazole	Diesel
La jauge à huile	Oil dip stick
La bougie (=candle)	Spark plug
Le piston	Piston
Le cylindre	Cylinder
Le carter	Sump
La soupape	Valve
Le radiateur	Radiator
La courroie de ventilation	Fan belt
La roue de secours	Spare wheel
La roue	Wheel
L'enjoliveur (m)	Wheel hub
La tête de delco	Distributor cap
La batterie	Battery
Le pare-brise	Windscreen
La lunette arrière	Rear windscreen
Le cric	Jack
Le feu de détresse	Warning/distress lights
L'essuie-glace (m)	Windscreen wiper
Le pneu	Tyre
Le pneu neige	Snow tyre
Le pneu clouté	Studded tyre

La boîte à gants	Glove box
La serrure de portière	Door lock
La vitre	Window
Le pot d'échappement	Exhaust pipe
L'amortisseur (m)	Shock absorber
Le permis de conduire	Driving license

Other driving expressions:

Conduire	to drive
Démarrer le moteur	to start the engine
Se mettre en marche (m)	to start moving
Changer de vitesse	to change gear
Rouler	to move forward
Dépasser	to pass
Accélérer	to accelerate
Doubler	to overtake
Freiner	to brake
S'arrêter	to stop

Chapter 9 – The doctor

Going to the doctor in France: What you need to know

Going to the doctor in France is a little bit different. The doctor himself (or herself) will greet you in the waiting room instead of a nurse calling your name and doctors here rarely wear the traditional white doctor coats we're used to seeing in the US. Keep that in mind.

More or less, going to the doctor in France is the same as in the US. You make an appointment, you go see the doctor, he/she examines you, diagnoses you, gives you a prescription if necessary, and you're on your way. I said MORE OR LESS the same. There are some nuances you might want to take note of if you're **going to the doctor in France**. Let's take a look.

Making the appointment

When you call the CABINET MÉDICAL to make an appointment, you will talk to the secretary who may or may not be in a good mood.

Phrase to use:

"Je voudrais prendre rendez-vous s'il vous plaît." (I'd like to make an appointment please).

Upon arrival

Normally you don't fill out 10 papers for insurance/new patient forms when going to the doctor in France like you would in the US, so don't show up early for paperwork. Doctors all over the world run late and it's not specific to France, but I must say no one is ever on time here. Upon arrival, let the secretary know you're there and if there's no secretary, go to the SALLE D'ATTENTE (waiting room) for your particular doctor. In most cases, the door will be marked as such and in a practice with multiple doctors, again go to the waiting room for your particular doctor.

Greet everyone in there with a "bonjour" and then sit down. The doctor will personally come and call you when it's your turn. There is no nurse visit to check your vitals or get your history first.

At the appointment

When going to the doctor in France, you'll first be asked by the doctor to present your carte vitale (insurance card) and to pay (this can also be done at the end). If you don't yet have your carte vitale, you'll get a *feuille de soins* (health form/receipt) to submit yourself to the **sécurité sociale**.

Once that's out of the way, you'll explain why you're there and the doctor will fully examine you. There's no nurse who comes to see you in advance, so be thorough.

Common dialog:

Cabinet du docteur Philippe, bonjour./ *Good morning, Doctor Philip's Clinic.*

Bonjour, excusez-moi de vous déranger, je voudrais prendre rendez-vous avec le docteur Maxime s'il vous plaît. /*Good morning, sorry for disturbing you. I wanted to make an appointment with Doctor Philipe, please.*

Quelles sont vos disponibilités ? (=quand ?)/ *When would you like to make an appointment?*

Je préfère mercredi matin. OU Tous les jours après 17h. OU Le plus tôt possible. OU Tout me va./ *I prefer Wednesday morning. OR any day after 5pm. OR As early as possible. OR Anything will do.*

Je vous propose le jeudi 12 à 10h./ *Is Thursday the 12 at 10 am convenient?*

Merci beaucoup, c'est très bien./ *That's good. Thank you very much.*

OU – Non, je ne suis pas disponible ce jour-là. Avez-vous autre chose (à me proposer) ?/ *No, I'm busy on that day. Could you suggest another vacant time slot?*

Vous pouvez me laisser votre nom ?/ *Could you give me your name?*

Tout à fait. (Say your name)/ *Certainly. (Your name)*

If it is urgent

C'est une urgence, est-ce que vous pourriez me prendre plus tôt ?/ *It's urgent, can you please give me an appointment at the earliest?*

Non, désolé. Tout est plein./ *No, sorry. We are full.*

Est-ce que vous auriez un autre collègue à me recommander ? J'ai absolument besoin de voir quelqu'un./ *Can you suggest any other doctor? I desperately need to see one.*

Oui./Non./ *Yes./No.*

If it is very urgent :

Est-ce que je dois me rendre aux urgences ?/ *DoI have to go to the E.R?*

Oui./Non./ *Yes./No.*

Merci madame/monsieur, à bientôt./ *Thank you, Madam/sir.*

Note:

You don't require your French papers to visit a doctor or the emergency ward.

You have to pay the full consultation fee and the bill for the medicines.

Don't forget to ask for the price when you book!

If you can't afford to pay the gynecologist's fee, go to Planning Familial.

Emergency French phrases:

You may come across an operator who speaks English but there is no guarantee of this. If you do not speak French, it is best to find a French-speaker whom you can trust.

- Police: La Police Nationale or gendarmerie
- Fire brigade: Les sapeurs pompiers
- Emergency services/ambulance: Service d'Aide Médicale d'Urgence or SAMU
- Poisoning emergency: Centre antipoison
- Road emergency services: Services d'urgence routière
- Emergency numbers: Numéros d'urgence
- It's an emergency: C'est une urgence.
- My name is…: Je m'appelle…
- My telephone number is…: Mon numéro de téléphone est le…
- I live at…: J'habite à…
- Help!: Au secours !
- Ambulance: une ambulance; J'ai besoin d'une ambulance. (I need an ambulance.)
- Heart attack: une crise cardiaque; Mon mari fait une crise cardiaque. (My husband had a heart attack.)
- Stroke: une attaque cérébrale; Je pense que ma femme a souffert d'une attaque cérébrale. (I think my wife suffered a stroke.)
- Choke: s'étouffer; Mon bébé s'étouffe. (My baby is choking.)
- Difficulty breathing/gasping: haleter or difficulté à respirer; J'ai du mal à respirer. (I have difficulty breathing.)
- To bleed: saigner; Je saigne beaucoup. (I am bleeding a lot.)

- Hemorrhage: une hémorragie; Mon mari fait une hémorragie. (My husband had a hemorrhage.)
- Concussion: une commotion cérébrale; Mon enfant est tombé. A-t-il une commotion cérébrale ? (My child fell. Does he have a concussion?)
- Diabetic: diabétique; Je suis diabétique. J'ai besoin d'insuline. (I need insulin).
- Labor: accouchement/accoucher; Ma femme accouche; la poche des eaux a percé. (My wife is giving birth. Her water has broken.)
- To be poisoned: s'empoisonner; Mon enfant s'est empoisonné. (My child has been poisoned.)

Headaches, colds, sore throat

Je tousse.

I have a cough.

Vous auriez quelque chose contre la toux ?

Do you have medicines for cough?

Toux grasse ou toux sèche ?

Do you have a cough with mucus or dry? (They often ask it)

J'ai mal à la tête. / Vous pourriez me donner quelque chose contre le mal de tête ?

I have a headache. / Can you give some medicines for headaches?

J'ai un rhume.

I have a cold.

Je me mouche tout le temps. / J'ai le nez qui coule.

I have a running nose.

J'éternue tout le temps.

I sneeze all the time.

J'ai mal à la gorge.

I have a sore throat.

J'ai la gorge très sèche.

I have a parched throat.

J'ai des glaires.

I have mucus.

J'ai de la fièvre.

I have a fever.

Pharmacy:

The pharmacist is called le pharmacien here. And a pharmacy is called la pharmacie. There are pharmacies everywhere, and you find them by looking for a big green cross. It is usually a big neon sign. They are open during the day, like other French shops. In case you need any special medication that cannot wait till the morning, you have to find une pharmacie de nuit, also called pharmacie de garde, which would be open at night.

The pharmacist sells the medicines.

Ask for a doctor:

Est-ce que je dois aller voir un médecin ?

SHOULD I SEE A DOCTOR?

Est-ce que vous avez un médecin à me recommander ?

DO YOU HAVE A DOCTOR TO RECOMMEND?

Vous avez son numéro ?/ MAY I HAVE THE PHONE NUMBER OF THE DOCTOR YOU RECOMMEND?

Vous avez quelque chose contre les allergies ?/ DO YOU HAVE MEDICINES FOR ALLERGY?

Medicine <u>Vocabulary</u> :

UN CACHET a tablet

UN COMPRIMÉ a pill

UNE PASTILLE a lozenge

ASPIRINE aspirin

LE DOSAGE the dosage

UNE GOUTTE a drop

LE MÉDICAMENT the medicine

UN PANSEMENT a bandage

PRESCRIRE to prescribe

ORDONNANCE the prescription

Conclusion

The first few times you try to speak French, you'll probably get it wrong. Your interlocutor won't be able to understand what you mean but it is okay, calm down. Relax. You're here for the trip and this book will help you with some survival French expressions.

Learning French is easy, but most of the time you will have to talk to native speakers, and they don't articulate that much, so you've got to listen carefully. But you'll get used to it with time.

You'll improve day by day, don't give up.